Under The Grittin's Wing
(A Norwich life)

Frederick G.G. Cobb

By Leeco Publications
leecopublications@outlook.com
©2020 Leeco Publications.

First published 2020

ISBN: 978-1-9163564-0-5

Acknowledgements and thanks to:

Great Eastern Railway Society (www.gersociety.org.uk) and their Files Emporium:

(https://www.gersociety.org.uk/index.php/home/sales/files-emporium-2) for permission to reproduce photographs and articles from the *LNER Magazine*.

Norfolk County Council's Library and Information Service's '*Picture Norfolk*' for permission to reproduce photographs.

Archant Limited and the Archant Library for permission to reproduce photographs and articles from their newspapers.

Alan Taylor for the front cover artwork.

Foreword

Frederick George Goodson Cobb (Fred) was born in Norwich in 1896. Apart from military service in World War One and a ten year 'exile' in Ipswich, he lived his entire life in Thorpe, Norwich.

He retired in 1961 after a fifty year career with the railways — initially the Great Eastern Railway (GER) which merged to become part of London and North East Railway (LNER) in 1923 and finally part of British Railways after nationalisation in 1948.

One of his main hobbies was writing and between 1929 and 1937 he was a regular contributor to the *London & North Eastern Railway Magazine*. Following his retirement, he contributed a number of articles of local interest to the *Eastern Daily Press* and *Eastern Evening News*. "Whiffler", a columnist in the *Eastern Evening News*, once described him as a writer of "no mean journalistic ability" and "a really good writer" — these words of commendation encouraged him in 1973 to write this autobiography.

Fred died in 1977 at the age of 80.

Contents

Preface   5

Chapter 1   Mother and Father   7
Chapter 2   Early Recollections   14
Chapter 3   The Shorthand Clerk   25
Chapter 4   World War I – England, May 1914–May 1916   34
Chapter 5   World War I – France, May 1916–October 1917   60
Chapter 6   World War I – Italy, October 1917–January 1918   81
Chapter 7   World War I – France, January 1918–January 1919   88
Chapter 8   Civilian again   95
Chapter 9   Back to Work 1919   98
Chapter 10   The Golden Years   107
Chapter 11   Bachelor Fred and the Broads   121
Chapter 12   Family Matters   130
Chapter 13   LNER and Mr Pettit   137
Chapter 14   LNER and Mr Wilson   159
Chapter 15   Out and About with LNER   166
Chapter 16   World War II   172
Chapter 17   LNER and back in Norwich   182
Chapter 18   LNER to Retirement   186
Chapter 19   Sentimental Journey   192

Appendix   Selection of articles written for the *London
             & North Eastern Railway Magazine*   201

Preface

In the late autumn of 1916 I was a young soldier of 19 years of age, and, looking out of the window of an attic of a château in northern France, I was attracted by the view of the gardens below and decided to make a sketch of them to remind me of the miracle of fate that had brought me from the dangers and rigours of trench warfare to the comparative safety and comfort of the headquarters of 11th Army Corps Headquarters of the British Expeditionary Forces in France, under the command of Lieutenant-General Sir Richard Haking, CB, KCB, KCMG.

I could never have imagined that more than 50 years later, that sketch, which had laid undisturbed for years, would give me a strong desire to visit those gardens, the lake and grotto, or what might be left to them after the ravages of two world wars.

It was when I found myself comfortably seated in a train at Norwich Thorpe station, not long since, bound for the village in France where I had spent almost two years in the First World War, that I decided to write the memoirs which I leave behind as a token of love and gratitude to my dear wife Irene for her love and understanding during our 50 years of married life.

The Griffin's wing was the emblem of the Great Eastern Railway on which revered line my father served for 47 years. In 1961 I completed 50 years' railway service with the GER, the LNER, and British Railways.

5

The garden of a chateau in Northern France.
A sketch by the author in 1916

Chapter 1 — Mother And Father

My father was born in 1861 in the small agricultural village of Worstead, Norfolk, which was once a flourishing town, made famous throughout the land when Flemish weavers settled there in the reign of Henry 1 (after Flanders had been inundated) to make their cloth which they named Worsted.

The only evidence of its former greatness is the beautiful church with its lofty embattled tower, built by prosperous wool merchants in the 14th century. I can remember my father saying the pews were separately boarded so that the congregation could sleep throughout the sermon and boys could play cards without being seen by the parson.

John, my father, started work on the Great Eastern Railway at Worstead station as a signalman and general boss (his words) when he was 18 for fourteen shillings a week. There were no elaborate devices for working the signals and closing the points, it had to be done by hand and the lever hung on to until the last coach had passed, and the signalman had to work from a hut instead of a modern signal box. His most exciting experience whilst at Worstead was the terrific blizzard which lashed the country on January 18th 1881 and covered it with great depths of snow with drifts up to the tops of hedgerows. Between North Walsham and Worstead a passenger train was blocked up in a snowdrift and it took the combined efforts of eight engines coupled together and acting like a snow plough to clear the line. Such was the force of that "battering ram" that an engine and tender were propelled into a field at Tunstead.

When he was twenty one he was promoted to signalman at Lakenheath station and received the princely sum of eighteen shillings a week. He thought it was a great achievement, but little did he know at the time that it would be the most important milestone in his life, for in the village there dwelt Mary Ann Elizabeth Steele, a young girl of fifteen and, you may have guessed, she eventually became his bride and my mother. She was born at Weeting, Norfolk, where unpretentious pits named Grimes Graves bear silent evidence of the existence of a considerable colony of flint workers who fashioned axes, spear heads, picks, hammers, fishhooks and other stone implements in the Early Stone or Neolithic Age. She had two brothers, Frederick and George, both of whom I was named after,

Father was 21 when he was promoted to Lakenheath

which makes me feel I have inherited a little part of the peace and harmony of that lovely village. Her father was the village blacksmith but bore no resemblance to the mighty man who stood under the spreading chestnut tree.

He often stood under the big walnut tree that grew in his front garden, it is still standing 100 years after. He was slight of build and mild of manner, which description also fits my grandmother who looked after the Post Office, which occupied the front room of their house.

The village was part of the estate of the squire who lived with his family and a retinue of servants at Weeting Hall, a large mansion standing in extensive parkland which also enclosed the village church. There were well tended gardens too, for I seem to remember being told that the squire's daughter caused quite a stir in the village when she married the son of the head gardener.

Mother used to tell us how the women curtsied, and the men touched their caps when the squire and his family drove

Weeting Post Office where mother was born

through the village street in a carriage drawn by four horses, and with two footmen in powdered wigs sitting stiffly behind. The village folk were not vassals but self-respecting

individuals displaying a reverence for a benefactor who had their interests very much at heart. He was generous in thought and deed, distributing blankets and other gifts at Christmas time and when my grandfather had to have his leg amputated as the result of a kick from a horse the squire made arrangements for him to be sent to a London hospital for the operation and paid all expenses. By a strange twist of fate my grandmother knelt on

Mother's parents
(both minus a leg)

9

some cinders, and, medical science not being what it is today, she was sent to a London hospital where her leg had to be amputated, again at the squire's expense.

As a result of these misfortunes my mother was sent to Lakenheath where she was brought up by her aunt and uncle who were childless, He was a land surveyor and a devout Christian.

It could not have been easy for John, the young railway signalman, to meet Mary, the young protege of a local preacher, in that village where a newcomer remained a foreigner for years and they could not have spent much time together as he worked twelve hours every weekday and also on a Sunday. Lakenheath station and the cottage where he lodged were three miles from the village which could only be reached by walking along a rough road with deep ditches on either side which separated it from the vast stretches of flat fen lands. The villagers extinguished their candles and oil lamps early every night. There were no lights in the street and the walk back to the station was a hazardous exercise in the dark as my father found out when he completely lost his sense of direction in dense fog and found himself struggling in the green slimy mud of a deep ditch. He clambered out and presented himself at the door of his lodgings only to be ordered by the elderly landlady to take off his trousers before he came indoors. She took them from him and hung them up on a hook in the ceiling of the living room usually reserved for a pig's carcase.

He would have suffered that and much more to have remained at Lakenheath, but his master promoted him to Yarmouth Vauxhall station as a higher-grade signalman at twenty shillings a week. Soon after taking up his duties the signalman's hut was dispensed with and he had the distinction of being the first to operate a signal box equipped with up-to-date mechanism for the new working of right-of-way signals. The move from Lakenheath carried with it very interesting work, but he longed for Mary to share his life and it was not long before he wrote to her uncle for his consent to their marriage. The uncle thought she was too young but could not have been too adamant for they were married at

The author's parents. "A contented couple

Lakenheath Church on March 31st 1885. He was 24 and she was 18 and what a marvellous married life it turned out to be. There was the perfect combination of a benign and devoted grandfather on my father's side and the Christian influence of a devout local preacher with the fortitude of a blacksmith and his wife on my mother's side.

Never once did any of their children hear a word of discontentment or anger creep into their sublime lives.

Their family of two boys (Reginald John [1895] and I [1896]) and two girls (Rosie Elizabeth [1890] and May Lilian Gladys [1899]) were born after they moved to Norwich where, for nearly thirty eight years, father was a ticket collector at Thorpe station and rose to be chief of the service.

He was a familiar figure at the barrier, known and liked by a considerable number of the travellers both from the City of Norwich and from the county. Travellers plied their wares by rail, their samples being packed in huge hampers;

Family portrait 1913.
May, the Author, Father, Rose, Reg and Mother

corn merchants attended the Corn Exchange in London regularly every Monday, directors and representatives of important firms had traders season tickets. Hundreds of sedentary workers swarmed into Thorpe station from dormitory towns like Cromer, Sheringham, North Walsham, Wroxham and Brundall. They were on their way to their offices and shops and when their day's work was done, you could see them streaming down Prince of Wales Road at the same time every afternoon on their way to catch their trains home. The railway was like one big hub and it prospered. I remember my father coming home one day and telling us the late Lord Kimberley came from London by train with a friend and walked over to the barrier specially to introduce the friend to him and added "This is the fellow I was telling you about, don't you agree he's the very image of Sir John Redman?" John Redman was famous at the time as the Irish Leader. The travelling public seemed to appreciate my father's cheerfulness and courtesy and treated him generously for he was for ever receiving rabbits, hares, pheasants and poultry. The gifts helped to keep us well-nourished and made it possible for him to buy a new house in Beatrice Road, Thorpe Hamlet which we moved into when I was five years of age. He worked 72 hours per week plus 12 hours on alternate Sundays for which he was paid twenty two shillings and six pence per week.

He was blessed with an industrious and loving wife who made our clothes on an old hand sewing machine which is still in my possession and is a visible reminder of her unselfish devotion. Father had a generous nature which he could not indulge as much as he would like. Many times, as we were just about to finish our tea, he would, without warning, throw a handful of pennies under the table for us to scramble after on our hands and knees. It gave him a lot of pleasure to see us "bumping" and "boring" as we tried to pick up as many pennies as we could.

Chapter 2 — Early Recollections

"There is a divinity that shapes our ends, rough-hew them how we will"
Pope

The earliest recollection of my childhood was when we lived in View Terrace, Victoria Road, off St. Leonards Road, Thorpe Hamlet*. Our house had uninterrupted views of the city of Norwich spread out below. Just beyond the front garden were the sandy slopes of a worked-out pit which made an excellent playground. At the bottom was a dumping ground where we children dare not venture as it was frequently patrolled by an old man, nicknamed 'Mun'. Mun with his black dog, chased off the boys who used to crawl through a hole in the fence when they came out of Thorpe Hamlet school, which was opposite, and toboggan down the sandy slope on old tea trays which they picked off the dump. If they saw Mun and his dog approaching they would scamper off through the fence yelling as they ran "Mun, Mun... a ton".

Strange to relate, that dump, in 1908, became known throughout Great Britain and beyond its shores, by sportsmen as "The Nest" the home of Norwich City Football Club. Very few people who had seen that unsightly and neglected pit, hemmed in on two sides by rows of cottages and sandy hills on the other sides, would have believed it could be transformed into a football ground capable of holding 20,129 spectators (with a very great squeeze). This was then the record gate when Norwich City played the famous amateur club, the Corinthians, in the F.A. Cup in

---

Victoria Road has since been renamed Guelph Road.

14

The Nest, Norwich. View Terrace is top centre of the picture.

the season 1928/29. Norwich City were outplayed and beaten by five goals to nil. I was in the crowd and it was a miracle nobody was hurt; the crush was so great it was impossible to raise an arm to get a handkerchief out of one's pocket.

To find sufficient space for the playing pitch, tons of sand were dug out of the slope where we had played as children leaving the sheer face of a cliff which had to be supported by a high concrete wall built to within a few feet of the pitch. I shall never forget November 15th 1919 when Tom Batey, a City player, broke his leg. A sharp crack like the snapping of a dry stick reverberated off the wall and stunned the spectators into silence.

The highlight of the football era at the Nest before the First World War was the famous 3–1 F.A. Cup victory over Sunderland on January 14th 1911 when Norwich City moved their brilliant full back, Billy Hampson, to centre forward and he scored two goals that moved the crowd to such a frenzy of joy and abandon that I saw hard hats thrown into the air never to be recovered. I guarantee that

15

no person present at that match who is fortunate enough to be alive today will ever forget that memorable afternoon.

There was more than a sandpit to remind me of the first five years of my life in the house upon the hill. There was the companionship of my next-door neighbour, George Ransom, three months my junior who shared most of my experiences. One day a swarthy Italian appeared in our cul-de-sac with a huge Russian bear which he led by a heavy chain attached to the collar around its neck. When the man chanted some unintelligible song, the bear danced until a copper or two had been collected and then man and beast moved on. That unusual spectacle stirred the instincts of George and me into action and after we had found two empty sacks and some rope, we co-produced our own dancing bear act, at the age of four years and a bit. George stepped into one of the sacks and pulled it up to his waist, he put the other sack over his head and the top half of his body, I tied the rope round his middle and there was a four feet high "Russian" bear bursting to dance. I led him up and down the cul-de-sac chanting "Alla-von-chee, Von-chee, Von-chee" which was something like the dancing song of the Italian. The "bear" danced, I held out my cap for alms, but we did not collect even enough to buy ourselves a farthing's worth of Mrs Lincoln's famous toffee.

Every youngster who lived in Thorpe Hamlet (especially those who lived in the roads that Mr Isaac Bugg Coaks, the Charlie Clore* of the 1890s, had named after his daughters Ethel, Ella, Marion, Florence, Beatrice and Primrose) has walked up Malvern Road and knocked on the back door of old Mrs Lincoln's terrace house, and asked for a "farnter" or a "ha'porth" of her toffee. She made it herself, broke it up into lovely brown lumps which she put into little screwed-up pieces of paper. 1 have never tasted better toffee in my whole life.

Sometimes we watched as the Norwich Snapdragon came rushing along the roads as fast as the man inside could run.

---

*Sir Charles (Charlie) Clore was a British property investor and developer who achieved a degree of publicity in the 1960s and 1970s.

It was followed by a crowd of children who yelled as they ran "Snap, Snap, steal the boy's cap" as the Snapdragon made efforts to peck off the caps' of the boys nearest to him. It is now in hallowed retirement in the Norwich Castle Museum.

There was peace and fraternity in our terrace and family friendships were cemented which lasted a lifetime. There was not, however, peace on earth, for I remember George and I trotting up and down the road singing with youthful glee a song about the Boer War which went something like this: -

Lord Roberts and Buller,
Baden Powell and White,
All went out to South Africa.
To have a jolly good fight,
And when the war is over,
How happy we'll be,
Our flag will fly over Pretoria,
And Kruger will hang on a tree.

We knew nothing about, the tragic implications of war.

We moved to our new house in Beatrice Road when I was five years of age. I seem to remember we paid around £200 for it (it would probable fetch £6,000 to £7,000 today)*.

George and his family moved just opposite about the same time and we were inseparable at school and play. One evening in 1908 we were collecting round pebbles from the roads for my father to make a cobbled pathway in the back garden. This will give some idea of the road surfaces in those days before John Macadam revolutionised road construction with his tar macadam.

A lady living in the next road opened her front door and beckoned us over to enquire if we would buy some eggs for her at a shop some distance away. Naturally we agreed to do so and although she had never seen us before she trusted us with a golden half-sovereign. The shopkeeper had sold out of eggs, but he would have some the next morning. When we had so informed the lady and given her back the half-

*In 2019 similar properties were being advertised for £220,000.

Beatrice Road, Thorpe Hamlet

sovereign, I volunteered to fetch them for her the next morning and my offer was gladly accepted. It was summer school holiday time and when I arrived at the house with the eggs, I was given all sorts to chores to do, sweeping the coconut matting in the kitchen on my hands and knees using a short brush and dustpan, doing the same to the carpets in other rooms after sprinkling tea leaves on them to lay the dust, cleaning knives and forks and running errands. I had never done any housework before, there were two girls in our house, to help my mother if needs be, and brother Reg who was one and a half years my senior, used to clean the knives and forks every Saturday morning for which he received an extra ha'penny a week. The steel knives were cleaned on a knife board with bath brick and elbow grease and the endless rubbing wore them thin and sharp. The steel forks were cleaned with a damp cork dipped in vinegar. It was a boon and a blessing to boys when stainless steel was invented.

I was a willing lad and just did as I was told. I was quite happy with the new experience and I am sure my unex-

18

pected arrival on the domestic scene in the corner house at the quiet end of the next road to mine was like a gift from heaven for Mrs Carrie Hemmings, the wife of Sammy Hemmings, a tenor of the Norwich Cathedral choir. She had just let her drawing room and the large bedroom above it to a young gentleman who had come to Norwich to take up an appointment as second brewer at Steward, Patteson, Finch & Co., a local brewery. Carrie, a short, plain looking woman, worked hard all day and well into the evening to supplement the salary of £60 per annum which the ecclesiastical authorities paid her husband for his vocal services. Sammy reminded me of Mr Pickwick, short, stout and of neat appearance. He used to look at me with kindly eyes from behind gold rimmed spectacles, but his kindness never reached his pocket to give me the smallest of coins. I expect he thought I was getting enough money for a youngster of my age and come to think of it I should not be surprised if I had more money to spend on myself than he had. I had become Carrie's right hand 'man' for which she paid me one shilling and six pence per week. Mr Bell, the young brewer, realised my potential and decided to give me two shillings per week plus a five shillings per quarter bonus if I gave satisfactory attention to his needs which were soon tantamount to the duties of a valet-cum-waiter. I thought he was one of nature's perfect gentlemen, he moved in the highest social circle, had a complete expensive wardrobe, wined and dined well, always read The Tatler, The Field, Punch, The Times and Bob Severs 'Pink Un' and was generous to a fault. His rooms were *hi sanctum sanctorum* he usually summoned me by pressing a bell button and I was always ready to carry out his wishes.

Carrie intruded on his privacy but once a day when she went to enquire what he wanted in the way of meals or to receive payment for his room and service. He would entertain his friends to lunch or dinner and the latter meal would often entail the preparation of six or more courses with no expense spared. It soon became my responsibility to lay the table, see that an adequate supply of claret, whisky, port, crème-de-menthe and other drinks were at hand, fill the silver cigarette box and renew the candles in the candle-sticks.

When I was satisfied that everything was ready for the guests, I would help Carrie in the kitchen until a bell rang to tell us dinner could be served. Dressed in a little white jacket which had been specially made for me, I carried in each course as the meal progressed. It was a solemn and serious occasion for me, unobtrusively waiting on those cultured young diners in the room illuminated only by the shaded light from the candles in the candlesticks standing on the dining table. The guests included regular officers from the Norfolk Regiment stationed at Britannia Barracks, young professional gentlemen, many of whom had taken over the family businesses from their departed fathers, fellow brewers and, most important of all for Mr Bell, his chief, Sir George Morse and Lady Morse. Sir George Morse was Mayor of Norwich in 1899 and again in 1922–23.

It was often late at night before I got home which was a matter of concern to my mother who thought Carrie was taking advantage of my good nature. I would explain it was a special occasion and I did not mind in the least. While all that entertaining was going on in the house Sammy would be quietly playing draughts in the living room with an old neighbour. He never helped in any way and only came into the kitchen to kiss his wife goodbye when he went off to the Cathedral services or to get her to tie his bow when he dressed up for an occasional singing engagement which usually earned him a guinea. Carrie seemed to accept this as a natural marital procedure and as long as she could recharge her batteries with a glass of beer from the barrel in the cupboard under the stairs to which Mr Bell had given her free access, she could go on for ever.

On a normal day I started at 7.15am cleaning knives, forks and shoes in a shed in the back garden and regularly at 8 o'clock I went upstairs and took Mr Bell a cup of tea and an apple, not forgetting the silver fruit knife. I would spread a rug on the carpet, draw out a round bath from under the bed (bathrooms being a rarity in Thorpe Hamlet in those days), go downstairs for two cans of water, one hot and the other cold, which I stood at the side of the bath with other necessary utensils ready for his morning ablutions. If he had had a good time the night before he would ask me to pour out a glass of Apenta Water which presumably was good for hang-overs. I would then dash to the Co-op butcher's in Rosary Road, sometimes for as little as three-pennyworth of shin of beef which I felt ashamed to ask for as my mother would never have sent me for such a small quantity. As it was, there was sufficient meat for that price to be 'dolled up' to make a decent lunch for Mr Bell, but he paid a good bit more for it. It was time to rush home for breakfast after that errand and then to school.

When morning lessons were over I rarely missed a game of football in the school playground with George and a few more like him before climbing over the school wall which was the quickest way of getting to Carrie's where I mashed the potatoes, set the lunch table, served the meal to Mr Bell, and then went home for my own dinner and then to school again.

It was the same drill every evening except when he dined out. Then I would lay out his dress clothes, dinner jacket or tails, white waistcoat, silk topper or opera hat, put gold-knobbed studs in his starched shirt front and have everything else ready for him. When he had left the house, I would put his day clothes away, with the trousers in the press, and when he went on holiday, I packed his travelling cases with never a complaint. He seemed to take what I did for granted and at twelve or thirteen years of age I had become an efficient valet, waiter and general help, which I think was, to say the least, an unusual achievement, for a lad of my tender years.

I am convinced it was not mere chance that Carrie Hemmings opened her front door when I was collecting pebbles but my destiny leading me to a situation where I could gain a wealth of experience that would enable me to meet the challenge of future years. I was contented with my work, my bank balance at the Norfolk & Norwich Savings Bank was religiously being enriched every week by two shillings and sixpence. I kept the odd shilling for pocket

21

money and the only thing that would have made me give it all up would have been if Carrie had refused to let me have Saturday mornings off when I told her I had been selected to play football for Thorpe Hamlet School. Wisely she agreed and the last season I played, which was 1910–1911, was the most successful and memorable. We won every game we played in Norwich, capturing the School League championship and the Bury Charity Cup, playing all the matches in the latter competition at 'The Nest' which was every budding footballer's ambition.

The last match of the season was the traditional "Champions versus the Rest of the League". This was played before the start of Norwich City's first team match (v Southampton) on April 1st 1911.

NORWICH SCHOOL LEAGUE.
CHAMPIONS (THORPE HAMLET) v. THE REST.

At the Nest.
Rest of the League (colours)—Barnes (Nelson Street), goal; Turner (Model) and Crowe (Nelson Street), backs; Todd, Vickers (Model), and Ramsbottom (Bull Close), half-backs; Pepper, Wilson (Nelson Street), Hagg (Model), Whittaker, and Douglas (Bull Close), forwards.
Thorpe Hamlet (white), Stroud, goal; Read and Allen, backs; Tooke, Stratton, and Knell, half-backs; Cobb, H. Chilvers, S. Chilvers, Ransome, and Le Fevre, forwards.
Referee—A. D. C. Sawford.

Eastern Evening News — Friday March 31st 1911

Courtesy of the Archant Library

The Champions, Thorpe Hamlet, continued their winning form and I scored the only goal. The *Eastern Evening News Football Edition** on April 1st 1911 said:

Although printed on pink paper it was not named 'The Pink Un' until 1913.

"Thorpe Hamlet may be accounted somewhat lucky to defeat the Rest of the League by 1–0 for the latter well merited a draw and the goal scored early partook of the nature of a gift, owing to a faulty goal kick, the only blemish on Barnes sterling display in goal. The knowledge of the game displayed by the participants was an agreeable revelation to the thousands of spectators who watched the match. The juvenile element gave vocal evidence of their presence and preference in no uncertain manner. Stroud's good work in the Hamlet goal was heightened by the sturdy kicking of Read, who would do well, however, to restrain a tendency to 'play to the gallery'. Knell's neat and clever work at left-half was the subject of much favourable comment. Stratton and Tooke proved sound tacklers. The younger Chilvers was very prominent up forward, his brother being too prone at times to endeavour to play the whole League defence on his own. Le Fevre was noticeable for some good work at outside left. Cobb was closely watched.

Barnes' display for the losers has already been commented upon. Turner at back was prominent throughout, and his partner, Crowe, after a shaky start, gave nothing away. Ramsbottom at left half gave Cobb little scope. Vickers, at centre half, shone, and Todd completed a sound trio. Whittaker and Douglas were the smartest wing on the field. Hagg lead the line well. Pepper was handicapped by the absence of Wilson."

This was a thrilling climax to my school days from which I emerged with two silver medals, a silver watch chain, a Malacca cane walking stick with silver embellishments from Mr Bell, and a green and yellow 'maize' vase from Carrie Hemmings. The vase is still in my possession.

I could not claim any success at Thorpe Hamlet School except a sound education in the three Rs and a knowledge of shorthand from my teacher. I may have held the record for length of school attendance as I started attending regularly at the age of two and a half years and left when I was fourteen and a half. I had passed my entrance examination for the Great Eastern Railway and my father decided, in his wisdom, I should stay at school to learn shorthand which accomplishment played a big part in my life during the next decade and, without it, as revealed in later pages, my young life might have expired on the battlefields of France. It is sad to record that 18,057 railwaymen were killed or died of wounds in the First World War.

Chapter 3 — The Shorthand Clerk

The great day dawned for me on May 11th 1911 when I joined the Great Eastern Railway at Norwich Victoria Goods station as a junior clerk at eight shillings a week. I was a proud lad when I walked into the station yard on that morning wearing my best suit, a five "bob" gun-metal case Ingersol watch in my pocket and sporting a silver watch chain on which hung my two football medals.

I buoyantly enquired of a little bearded man the way to the Goods Office and he escorted me to it and immediately told me what my duties were. It was about the only time I felt comfortable in his presence as he turned out to be the officious Chief Clerk and a strict disciplinarian. He had a mirror at eye level on the wall in front of his desk so he could see what we were doing at our desks behind his back. The staff worked quietly while he was in the office, but in his absence indulged in leg-pulling and harmless banter which spread to the outside staff and made my short stay at Victoria an enjoyable and memorable one.

Norwich Victoria Station

Courtesy Norfolk County Council

The Shorthand Clerk at 16 years of age

I soon found an outlet for my youthful zest, riding up and down the sidings in the luxury of a first class compartment while the carriages were being shunted. I would pull myself up into the compartment without being seen by the engine driver, gaze admiringly at myself in the mirrors and sink down into the comfortable seats which was something I knew I would not be able to do on a real train journey. My enthusiasm received a jolt one day when I realised the train had picked up speed and was on its way to Trowse. I jumped out without thinking of the consequences but fortunately it was only my pride that was hurt.

The Victoria Goods station has been fully closed since 1966 but the shed and bonded warehouse were, for a year or two afterwards, used as furniture showrooms. They have now been bull-dozed out of existence and nothing has been left to remind us of the important contributions the station made towards the prosperity of the industrial, commercial and family life of the City of Norwich. Lest the memory should be lost in the abyss of time I have recorded my happy experiences during the first year of my railway career.

At the station there was one Goods Agent who was also in charge of Norwich Thorpe station (Mr W.A. Lincoln, who many will remember as chairman of the Norwich Building Society in years past), a Chief Clerk and fourteen other clerks including one full time in the coal yard and another in the bonded warehouse. The warehouse also housed a Customs officer and his assistant, who saw to it that duty was paid on the huge quantities of whisky, port and other liquids liable to duty that passed in and out of bond. A number of staff of Coleman & Co. were permanently employed there making Wincarnis, advertised the world over as "The Wine of Life".

The outside staff comprised a foreman, checkers, yardmen, porters, horse shunters, horse drawn vehicle drivers, a weighbridge man and a stableman who looked after a dozen or more horses. All this staff was needed for the vast tonnages of foodstuffs, coal, raw materials and other traffic that arrived every day.

There was "B.H. Extra" butter for Butler & Hacon, all kinds of fruit from Covent Garden for wholesale merchants, carboys of acid for Boulton & Paul and Barnards wire netting industry, sugar and chocolate making supplies for A.J. Caley & Sons (now Mackintosh) to mention just a few that readily come to mind. The railways had the monopoly in transport, and they prospered.

One of my first jobs was to make out and deliver advice notes by hand to firms in the city. I got to know all the coffee carts where I could get a cup of coffee and a bun for a penny. I had a free bottle of mineral water at Caley's and often bought twelve big spotted oranges for a penny at W.H. Lacey & Sons, Grosvenor Road. I picked them out of a box where they had been thrown after sorting and soon discovered that even if the wrapping was "mushy" the orange was sound.

With a satchel full of oranges, I would walk buoyantly to St. Giles Street where one of the young girls in Madame Lee's top-storey dressmaking rooms would see me and come down for a half dozen to share with my sister Rosie's work-girls, who would be waving gleefully from the window. They were happy, carefree days.

Incidentally it might be of interest to learn that as a dressmaker's apprentice my sister did not receive a penny in wages for two years, after which time she received the princely sum of two shillings and sixpence a week.

It was a historic occasion when the first motor fire engine arrived at Victoria station on a flat-bottomed wagon. It was a modest looking affair compared with the mechanical wonders of the present, but it created such an interest that Albert Pitchers, the bonds clerk, went home for his camera and photographed it with me sitting on it, which makes me the first person to sit on a motor fire engine in Norwich. It played a very significant part in the disappearance of all horse-drawn fire engines, in particular, and indeed in all horse-drawn vehicles in general.

There was another young lad in the office who had been in my class at Thorpe Hamlet School and had played with me since we were five years of age. He grew up with an obsession for "bullock wopping", going off alone every Saturday morning, carrying a thick stick, bound for "The Hill" — the name given to the Norwich Cattle market. He persuaded me to go with him on one occasion, and after the sales, I found myself following a large herd of bullocks through the city and into the country with him and the drover "wopping" the hindquarters of the unfortunate beasts to keep them on the right road. After a while I left them to carry on walloping and went home.

I imagine he got his craze from his father, who was Goods Agent at Trowse station, one of the largest cattle receiving stations in the country, where between 30,000 and 40,000 head of Irish steers were dealt with every year. They were driven through the busy streets of Norwich on Saturdays, to and from the market, and the bewildered beasts caused much confusion and commotion, sometime dashing on to pavements and into shops. There was talk of a bull entering a china shop in Magdalen Street and, happily, coming out without doing damage.

The bulk of the cattle arrived at Trowse between September and December each year. They were fattened on lush Norfolk pastures and "boxed" at farms in the winter destined to become "the good roast beef of old England". The "bullock wopping" lad was two days my senior — he started at Victoria on a Monday and I followed on Wednesday of the same week. That two days seniority proved an advantage to

Trowse Station circa 1913

Courtesy Norfolk County Council

him as he sat at a desk all day while I did the boy's jobs, running errands, pasting invoices in skeleton books, fetching and taking back heavy dusty files which were kept in a so-called book room under the goods platform. The book room must have been the filthiest filing room in the U.K. Heavy old books of invoices hung from six inch nails knocked into the wooden supports of the platform. Cobwebs were heavy with dust that had percolated through the floorboards of the platform and the place would have put 'Dirty Dicks' to shame. To get in or out a lad had to scramble through an opening four feet high which opened onto the side of the platform and so take the risk of being run over by a passing trolley.

I was happy doing the boy's jobs but not when the other lad who was two days my senior was given a week's leave of absence soon after he had joined the railway. His father wanted him to accompany him and his wife on holiday and pulled some strings in the District Office. Neither he nor I was entitled to a holiday until the following year and I was told I could not have one. I had not an influential father on the railway and it was not politic to protest as many a lad had found out to his cost. There were no unions to fight our cause in those days.

He had, however, nobody behind him the morning we were both summoned separately into the Goods Agent's office and tested in our efficiency as shorthand clerks. The Goods Agent had been asked to select a shorthand clerk for the District Goods Manager at Norwich Thorpe station and I was selected for the position. It was an entirely new experience for me in the District Office. The staff had a different approach to their work which had been brought about by the mastermind of the District Goods Manager, who, since his appointment in 1908, had weeded out those of his personal staff who had shown signs of inefficiency or of not bending to his will and word. They were packed off to stations and he had got together a team of young section chiefs who he trained to subservience and a high degree of efficiency. He was the nephew of Sir William Burt, a former General Manager of the Great Eastern Railway and had literally

Norwich Thorpe Station

Courtesy Norfolk County Council

been born with a railway manager's pen in his hand. Small of stature, aristocratic in appearance and address, he was a disciplinarian of the old Victorian order and ruled his 90 odd stations in the Norwich district with clinical efficiency.

I sat at a table in his office every morning, as quiet as a mouse, listening to him giving orders to his clerks and taking down letters at his dictation. It was excellent training for me. No person was allowed to enter his office until the Chief Clerk had decided he was of sufficiently high importance to enter the 'Holy of Holies'. It was almost as difficult to obtain an audience with him as, I imagine, it was with His Majesty King George V who was on the throne at the time.

For the outside staff it was an impossibility unless it was somebody unfortunate enough to have erred in the execution of his duties when he would be ordered to go up to Norwich to see Mr Hall, a dreaded summons. The latter held court in his spacious office on Saturday mornings and I would have to be at my table with notebook and pencil at the ready, not to take shorthand notes but, I suspected, to make the proceedings look more impressive.

One specific occasion has stayed in my thoughts since 1913 because I happened to look across the office and saw

31

real distress on the face of an honest looking country porter who was being castigated and humiliated for having cross-labelled two trucks which arrived at the wrong stations and had to be re-directed. I felt a sudden resentment at the severity of his remarks for a mistake which nowadays would be passed over by the management, if indeed it came to notice. The man's union would have something to say about it too, I imagine, but then it was only the District Officer's inborn desire for perfection in the Norwich district.

After my long training as a "valet" before I left school, it came naturally to me to attend to the needs of the District Goods Manager who found no occasion to reprimand me. In fact, he surprised me one day when he told me he had arranged for me to be temporarily attached to Trowse station so I could gain experience in all sections of Goods Office work. I was recalled after a few months when the work in the office had become heavy and resumed as a short-hand clerk until I volunteered for the army soon after the outbreak of the War in 1914 when I had reached my 18th birthday.

Typewriters were not in use on the railways and all reports and letters had to be written in copying ink, in one's best handwriting. A long but satisfying job for those who could write well and had a sense of the artistic. Copies were taken by placing the separate sheets between two moist pages in a copying book which was then squeezed in a heavy hand press.

A historic event was triggered off one Sunday morning by a knock on my front door. I had a mild shock when I opened it and saw the "Guvnor" standing outside. He asked me to go to his house in the afternoon with my shorthand notebook where he dictated a lengthy report to GER Headquarters recommending that Norwich Victoria station should be closed to passenger traffic.

There was no Beeching plan in those days and it took three years before Parliament finally passed the Bill autho-rising the closure to passengers in 1916, during which time I made my last journey from Victoria station in December 1914. It was in a troop train with 1,000 recruits of the

2nd/4th Battalion, Norfolk Regiment bound for an unknown destination which turned out to be Peterborough, and on the very day the station was closed, which was May 22nd 1916, I was in the trenches in Flanders.

For his work in connection with the closure, Mr Hall was congratulated by the Chairman and Vice-chairman of the Great Eastern Railway, which was a great honour.

Chapter 4 — World War 1
England, May 1914–May 1916

When war was declared on August 4th 1914, several of the clerks in the office were already in the Territorials — either in the 4th Norfolks, the 1/6th Norfolk Cyclists or the Norfolk Yeomanry and it was not long before they were called up. Others answered Lord Kitchener's call for 100,000 men to form his "Kitchener's Army". Those enlistments so depleted the ranks of the clerical staff of the Great Eastern Railway that the General Manager issued a decree that no more clerks would be allowed to join up.

I was too young and headstrong to be deterred by such an edict. I sat at my desk one morning and looked round at the empty desks of those who had joined up and made up my mind to go straight away to the Drill Hall and enlist in the Norfolk Regiment. I told the Chief Clerk what I was about to do but he was not at all sympathetic and that was the last I saw of the office for over four years.

The District Goods Manager told my father I had disobeyed orders and had prejudiced my chances of re-joining the railway, but they accepted me back after the war was over.

We had been drilling and "bobbing about like corks on the water", as our old-timer Sergeant Major described our marching efforts, for more than a month in Chapel Field Gardens when we were given a pair of army boots and a kit bag and told to report to the Drill Hall at seven o'clock the next morning with our personal belongings packed in the kit bag. The battalion was leaving Norwich for a secret destination. This was a sudden shock to my parents whose anxiety about my future well-being would have been lessened if they had known where we were going.

Sisters May (left) aged 15 years and Rose (right) aged 24 years in September 1914

My mother and sisters were up early the next morning to make sure I had a good breakfast and was well prepared for the journey. Father was at work and brother Reg in bed having bade me farewell upstairs. Our feelings seemed to be well under control as I said goodbye and they would have remained so, at least until I was out of the house, if sister Rose, my second mother, had not seen the button which was hanging loosely on my civilian overcoat and had decided to sew it on securely. It was when we saw the tears well in her eyes preventing her from threading the needle that the slender threads holding back our emotions suddenly snapped and I made a hurried exit from the house with the button still hanging and a strange feeling in my throat not uncommon to young soldiers leaving their loved ones for the first time. We had plenty of laughs about that little episode in later life.

Why the move was kept so secret is beyond comprehension. We were just a crowd of "rookies" and Kaiser Bill would not have been the least bit interested, particularly if he had seen us "marching" later on that day through the streets of Peterborough with no uniforms or rifles, struggling awkwardly with our heavy kitbags, to a field where we had to stand for more than four hours waiting to be allocated to billets. We were chilled to the bone as the bitterly cold wind seared through our totally inadequate civilian clothes and almost every one of us caught colds from that long and severe exposure. The second-in-command of our Company came on parade with a particularly bad cold and a hacking cough which seemed to almost double up his slender frame like a question mark. It was a blood red handkerchief which he brought up to his flushed face when he coughed that gave me concern for his state of health and made me feel he would go into a decline if he did not see a doctor. In spite of my youthful imagination he lived a long and active life. He was Lord Mayor of Norwich in 1926–27, he received a knighthood in the New Year's honours in 1938 for political and public services in this "no mean city" of ours and became world renowned as Sir Robert Bignold, chairman of the Norwich Union Insurance Societies. It is indeed remarkable what fifty odd years will do to a man's figure; in recent years a photograph which appeared in the local Press showed him to be a well-built, broad shouldered gentleman. He died in 1970 at the age of 78 years.

We were billeted on the inhabitants of Peterborough who received seventeen shillings and six pence per week subsistence allowance for each soldier. We were selected for our billets in alphabetical order and I was paired with young Chettleburgh whose Christian name escapes me at the moment. I had known him for a year or more as a clerk in the Telegraph Office at Norwich Thorpe station, so we had something in common as fellow railwayman, or railway "boys" perhaps I should have said, and our stay with a young married couple in Gladstone Road was very enjoyable. In the evening of our arrival we sat on a sofa in the tiny living room feeling tired and despondent after our hectic day and Alf, the young husband who worked for an engineering-firm, decided to cheer us up with some music on his Edison Bell phonograph. He put on a black, cylindrical shaped record which turned out to be the most inappropriate one he could possibly have chosen for the occasion. From a huge horn came the voice of a popular tenor singing with Irish fervency the pathetic and tear-jerking number entitled "Where is my wandering boy tonight". These words rekindled my emotions and brought back to me the sad parting from my mother and two sisters that morning and I pictured them at home asking themselves the same question. I had had enough for one day and went to bed early. It was sad that young Chettleburgh should be killed in action only two weeks after we landed in France in May 1916.

There was a serious shortage of war materials in the early months of the war and when at long last we were issued with uniforms we were very excited. We regarded each other appraisingly when we wore them on parade for the first time, but my enthusiasm waned when, in my leisure hours, I strolled through the small town. I missed the salutations and the glad eye glances that had been pleasing features of the walks with my chums when we passed through the friendly streets of Norwich. It soon dawned on me I was now just like a million others in uniform and these joyful rapports with the opposite sex were things of the past.

Middle Drive, Lowestoft 1915

The 2/4th Norfolk Regiment moved to Lowestoft in January 1915 and we were again billeted on the inhabitants. When six of us settled in at a house in the Middle Drive; the comfortably furnished dining/cum/sitting room with the sea view and the continuous sound of waves pounding and receding on the seashore gave us a pleasant awareness of the good fortune that had brought us from the drabness of wartime Peterborough to a fine seaside resort near our homes. We were welcomed by a little postman and his wife, a happy couple, who treated us like summer season visitors.

Our meals were well prepared, the bed linen was changed regularly, and we were in clover.

We paraded every morning in front of Claremont Pier, the salubrious ozone tanning our faces and turning our bright brass buttons green. It was soldiering on a grand scale, but it did not prevent us from becoming a well-disciplined and well-trained unit which every one of us who was lucky enough to come back from the war remembers with pride and pleasure. It was an easy task for our officers and non-commissioned officers to train those men who were mostly from the country and who had been brought up to respect authority and to accept hard work and leisure as the natural way of life. Their parents had taught them how to behave in the company of their "betters" who were usually the squire, the parson, the schoolmaster and even the station master. They were placid, responsive and excellent material for shaping into soldiers.

At weekends, fathers, mothers, sweethearts and friends flocked into Lowestoft to see their soldier boys; trains were filled, restaurants and teashops flourished. Everybody seemed to be happy.

We were a mixed bunch in our billet. There was the son of a Norfolk farmer and Billy Huke who had been a colleague of mine at Thorpe station. We got on well together. There was also a quiet little chap who we could not get to know much about except that he had worked in a Norwich shoe factory. He had bad feet and an awkward gait which was very noticeable when we were on the march. It was no surprise when he was discharged on medical grounds, the real surprise was how he got into the army in the first place.

The fifth member of our billet was the only son of parents living in the country, who could be included with the parson and the squire as one of the "better" families. Colonel Mornement, who had been given the task of raising the 2/4th battalion of the Regiment, had, in his wisdom, decided that one Company in the battalion should be formed from businessmen in the county of Norfolk and Sergeant R.H. Mottram, who interviewed every man as he arrived in the Drill Hall for the first time, had done a good job as far as our fifth member was concerned, in selecting him for "B" Company. He was a nice sort of chap, well-educated and all that, but we had the feeling he might not have felt so much at home in any of the other Companies as he had been too well nurtured, and we reckoned he had never cleaned a pair of boots in his life until he joined the army. He was a good enough soldier on parade but simply could not adapt himself to "spit and polish". When we sat together each evening after tea, cleaning our buttons and boots ready for parade the following morning, he would put on gloves before picking up his button stick, and the pink powder commonly known as 'soldiers friend', and with the swing of the brush would keep repeating in a cultured voice "I'm bored to tears". He left after a while to take a commission and no doubt his boredom disappeared when he was provided with a batman to do the menial work for him. Although he quickly passed out of our lives that oft-repeated remark became a catch-phrase with us. When asked how we were getting on we would invariably assume an exaggerated 'Oxford' accent and reply "I'm bored to tee-arrs". It did not truthfully express our feelings, but it gave us a lot of fun.

The sixth member of the billet had no sense of humour and gave himself airs. His failings showed up very clearly when the lady of the house served our meals.

We chatted to her and expressed appreciation, all except the odd man out, who accepted his meals as impersonally as if they had come from a vending machine. We had been fore-warned he was different, and we found this out the day our Platoon Sergeant ordered the senior soldier of each billet to go to the Quarter Master's Stores after tea to collect a tin of dubbin for the use of all the soldiers in his billet. Our sixth member happened to be the senior soldier and whilst we were having our tea, he boasted with indignation that he was not going to be an errand boy for the rest of us and insisted the youngest member should go, which happened to be me. I referred him to the Sergeant's specific order and refused to go. He went off to the Q.M. stores in a rage and later burst into our room holding a tin of dubbin with the lid off shouting "Here's your dubbin". I sat in a comfortable armchair and he advanced with the obvious intention of pushing the opened tin into my nose. I reacted quickly and threw myself at him to wrest the tin from his hand and give him a dose of his own medicine. We both landed on a sofa with a heavy bump that brought the little postman and his wife quickly up from the basement. We stopped as if by magic and sanity came back into the room. I had neither won nor lost the combat, but I was happy I did not lose the respect of the landlady and that of my fellow comrades. She told them afterwards she was glad I had deflated him. We carried on as though nothing had happened, but he got his own back a few weeks later by what I felt was a cruel act of fate.

One afternoon we were being dismissed from parade when the Sergeant told me in a casual sort of manner to report to the orderly room after tea. Just as I was about to start off a tropical storm broke over Lowestoft, with thunder, lightning, and torrential rain. I would have been wet through after only a few yards and waited for the storm to abate. I did not think it was very urgent and was still waiting when the 'sixth one' came in soaked through but excited to 'high heaven'. He had hardly got his breath back before he gasped that he was going to Norwich as a clerk at Division Headquarters. He would live at home with a seventeen shillings and six pence a week subsistence allowance and it was a permanent appointment. Then with a twisted grin he pointed a finger at me and said, "YOU would have gone if you had turned up at the orderly room". He happened to have gone to see the battalion doctor and was waiting in the orderly room for the rain to ease off before returning to the billet. It was time to close the orderly room and as I had not turned up, he was given the job.

I tried to look unconcerned, but it was the greatest disappointment of my life to have missed the chance of being re-united with my family all because of a thunderstorm. There would have been no more parades, drills, guard duties, route marches, sticking a bayonet into the sides of sacks filled with straw hanging on gibbets in a field, which we had to imagine were German soldiers, and my mother would have been paid seventeen shillings and six pence a week subsistence allowance which was nearly as much as my father had been able to give her to provide for a young family of four children. It was years before I could get it out of my system, but the effect of the blow lessened when I was selected months later for duty in a Brigade office and finally in Corps Headquarters. I realise now I would have missed a wealth of experience of human relationship, administrative work and of travel if I had hibernated in Norwich for the whole of the war.

The Commanding Officer, Lieutenant Colonel E.M. Mornement, CBE, TD, contributed the following account of the activities of the 2/4th Norfolk Regiment to the *History of the Norfolk Regiment, 1685–1918* at the request of the author F. Loraine Petre, OBE.

"In January 1915 the battalion moved to Lowestoft with orders to co-operate with the officer commanding Naval Base. An extensive system of fortifications was carried out on the North, South and West of the town and hard field training proceeded with.

Japanese 275 rifles were issued and 80,000 rounds of ammunition. A battery of 12 pounder field guns was allocated to the battalion by the officer commanding, Naval Base. Very remarkable efficiency in sea target practice was attained and the guns always accompanied the battalion on night operations. The battalion also provided the personnel for the naval searchlights and for the No. 2 Armoured train which operated on the railways of East Anglia.

During 1915 Lowestoft suffered severely from Zeppelin raids and casualties occurred among civilian inhabitants and the battalion. One boarding house in which 28 of the latter were billeted was demolished".

I remember that raid and to the best of my recollection there were, miraculously, no casualties to any of the 28 soldiers. Neither were there any the night I was on guard in the doorway of an empty shop in the Middle Drive opposite the Hatfield Hotel.

The sergeant of the guard was just telling me "there was a zeppelin about" when, without any warning of its approach the airship dropped a bomb on a boarding house nearby.

I saw another burst on the roadway less than a hundred feet from me and then some huge splashes rose up from the sea as the Zeppelin released the remainder of its bombs and made off back to Germany. One of our chaps ran out of the shop and fired a shot into the air from his Japanese rifle but he might as well just have used a pop gun.

I was surprised when I saw how small a crater the bomb made and more surprised still a few minutes later when the front door of the bombed house opened and Private Land and two other members of "B" Company came out looking like bewildered millers who had fallen into bags of flour. Their uniforms were covered with white dust from shattered ceilings. They were shaken but unhurt. There was an old lady in the house and she too was unhurt.

The first Zeppelin raid on Lowestoft was in the early morning of April 16th 1915 when three bombs were dropped. I looked out of my bedroom window and saw Latten's timber yard blazing fiercely. It was a close shave for the Naval Base, HMS Halcyon II, which was moored close by. Damage was done to house property near Lowestoft Central station and three horses belonging to the Great Eastern Railway were killed. It was fortunate that the bombs were small compared with those dropped in the Second World War but in spite of this there were distressing civilian casualties in later raids.

Colonel Mornement's reference to the No. 2 Armoured train takes me back to a day in the early Spring of 1915 when I read in Battalion Orders, Part 2, that volunteers were required for duty on an Armoured train including one soldier for clerical duties. As an erstwhile railway clerk, it was just made for me and very soon I found myself with a sergeant and twelve men at North Walsham, a Midland & Great Northern station where the train was based. We were accommodated in three bell tents standing in a meadow between the M & GN and GER stations. It was really too early in the year to be sleeping under canvas and the nights were cold, but we were young and the freedom from parades, route marches, kit inspections, and the like, more than compensated for a few shivers in the night. I did nothing but clerical work and not much of that. The others did guard duties and we all accompanied the train on its daily jaunts.

The composition of the train was one Great Western engine in the middle, one armour plated wagon coupled in front for the officers and one to the rear of the engine for other ranks. There was a twelve inch gun mounted on a flat top wagon at each end of the train. A captain of Royal Artillery and some gunners looked after the operations, although we never saw a shot fired or indeed wanted to. Lieutenant Turnbull, son of Sir Robert Turnbull, General Manager of the Great Western Railway, was in charge of train movements. The driver was a sergeant and the fireman a private in the Royal Engineers and were both enlisted railwaymen. We would steam along the North Norfolk coast and down the picturesque stretch from Cromer to Yarmouth Beach station where the railway line flanked the coast and deserted beaches for miles and miles. We always returned to North Walsham in the afternoon. There was one unforgettable and out of this world night ride when we chugged slowly over the same stretch and gazed admiringly at the vast expanse of countryside, our Norfolk heritage, looking so enchanting and beautiful in the bright moonlight and from the other side of the train we could see the spacious North Sea and the waves scintillating with light as they rippled over the yellow sands only a stone's throw from the railway line.

When the train travelled at full speed we were jolted up and down like Yo-Yos as we sat facing each other on wooden forms in the steel plated wagon. An engine driver, on permanent loan from the Great Eastern Railway Locomotive department at Norwich Thorpe, was attached to the unit for emergency operations if necessary. He always sat with us on one of the forms and was fond of telling us that the jolting was good for the kidneys. I found no lasting benefit from it and had a kidney removed some thirty years later, but that is another epoch in my life from which, by the Grace of God and my destiny, I was privileged to emerge to continue a happy and active life.

It was a red letter day for me when we pulled into the Royal Dock at Norwich Thorpe station. The railwaymen were excited as it was the first time many of them had seen an armoured train and when my former colleagues came down from their offices under the station clock, we had a very happy reunion.

After a stay of two months at North Walsham we went back to the 2/4th Norfolks at Lowestoft, refreshed by the change of scenery and routine, ready to enjoy a full summer at the seaside. I was billeted this time in the comfortable home of Mrs Mummery at Grand View on the Esplanade, a house which was destroyed on April 25th 1916 when a squadron of German battle cruisers bombarded the town.

She provided us with good meals in her spacious drawing room overlooking the sea. It was like being in a first class boarding house. I had a single bedroom to myself, a half a dozen splendid comrades including Bob Abbs, from Runton, who had a warm heart and a fine bass voice and Jimmy Curtis, a gentle, gangling, through and through Norfolk giant, whose father kept the bow fronted fruit shop near Cromer church. I cheerfully settled down to military training and discipline. Church parades were our "pièce de résistance" which we presented to the inhabitants of Lowestoft every Sunday morning with military music supplied by the regimental band.

The battalion assembled in columns of companies on the Royal Plain, officers, NCOs, and men faultlessly turned out waiting for our second-in-command, Major Edward Mann, who we now know as Sir Edward Mann of Thelverton Hall, to give the command to "Stand to attention". Then, as if with but one accord, bodies became erect, eyes alert and every soldier looked straight to his front as the stern and proud figure of our Colonel appeared before them mounted on a high charger. He would gaze intently along each rank from his high pedestal and when not a man stirred or an eyelid flickered he would give the order to march and majestically led us with our rifles at the slope and the band playing, through the town to St. Margaret's church. When the service was over we would pick up our rifles which had been stacked outside the church and the procession would ribbon its way back to the Royal Plain. As an extra entertainment for the onlookers and to flaunt the Colonel's ego we would march to attention along the Esplanade from Claremont Pier to the Royal Plain where we would stand stiffly to attention. Even the spectators seemed awed by the authority of that commanding little figure on horseback and the Royal Plain was as quiet and still as the Two Minute Silence on Armistice Day until his stentorian voice roared out "WHO IS THAT MAN IN *** COMPANY WHO MOVED HIS HEAD?"

When he had satisfied himself that every one of the thousand men below his gaze were as motionless as statues, he would dismiss us for the day.

On parade in Lowestoft

My uncle Fred, a railway signalman at Yarmouth Vauxhall station, came to see me one Sunday and stood with the silent onlookers. He was very impressed and his first words to me were "My word, partner, I've never seen you under control like that before".

We felt like actors rehearsing a pageant under the producer's critical eye. We were proud of the way we were shaping as soldiers and the impression we were making on

46

the Lowestoft people who had come to accept us as part of their way of life. When, later in the war, I saw French and Italian soldiers, in their respective countries, marching with slovenly gait, I appreciated more than ever the excellent training we received under Colonel Mornement and his ex-regular army non-commissioned officers.

I was very keen on swimming before I enlisted and had won several small club prizes and was delighted when I found there was an indoor swimming pool near my billet, the South Lowestoft Swimming Baths on London Road which several years later was converted into a cinema. The lessee and manager was Professor A.G. Cutts who helped to promote an interest in swimming amongst the 2/4th personnel. I was appointed a swimming instructor and still have the Instructor's Ticket dated May 28th 1915 which admitted me into the Baths free of charge and a cutting from the *Lowestoft Journal* giving an account of a Military Swimming Gala held on August 27th 1915 which attracted a large audience of civilians, soldiers and Naval Ratings from the Naval Base HMS. Halycon II. I was a competitor in the diving section and well remember the applause when each diver came to the surface after his competing dives. Professor Cutts judged the competition and selected three finalists. They were Company Quartermaster Sergeant Colls, Sergeant Gough and myself, all from "B" Company. We each had to dive from the high board, the springboard, the table and do a running dive off the side of the swimming pool. This was one of the rare occasions in the Army when a Private could gain an ascendency over a non-commissioned officer, without getting himself into trouble, and I was pleased to do just that by winning the diving championship.

To coin a phrase, everything was going along swimmingly at Lowestoft that summer and I doubt if any infantryman in Great Britain was training for active service overseas under more pleasant conditions. I liked the route marches best. They were not the blistering foot slogging on Salisbury Plain we endured the following year but for me they were sheer uninhibited pleasure because when we left the town behind us and marched "at ease" we sang lustily every marching

AUGUST 27, 1915.

MILITARY SWIMMING GALA AT LOWESTOFT.

On Wednesday afternoon a swimming gala in which men of the 61st Prov. Batt. (T.F.) took part (by kind permission of Lieut.-Col. Mornement and officers, who provided the prizes), was held at the South Lowestoft Swimming Baths, placed at disposal by Mr. A. G. Cutts, the popular lessee and manager, who made all arrangements and rendered yeoman service. Following are results of the contests:—

Breast Stroke.—1 Co.-Sergt.-Major Raymond, B Co.; 2 Pte. Shread, C Co.

Diving.—1 Pte. Cobb, B Co.; 2 Sergt. Gough, B Co.

Championship of Battalion.—1 Pte. Howard, C Co.; 2 Sergt. Gough, B Co.

Walking Race.—1 Pte. Eldeet, B Co.; 2 Corpl. Alderton, C Co.

Company Relay Race.—Winner, C Co.; team: Capt. Daynes, Pte. Willis, Pte. Long, Pte. Howard.

Obstacle Race.—1 Pte. Buck, D Co.; 2 Corp. Daynes, C Co.

Handicap Race.—1 Co.-Qr.-Mr.-Sergt. Colls, 2 Pte. J. Smith.

Team Race (four men aside).—H.M.S. Halcyon v. 61st Prov. Batt. Winners, H.M.S. Halcyon.

Officers' Race.—1 Lieut. Back, 2nd Sec.-Lieut. Banger.

At the conclusion the men gave three hearty cheers for Lieut.-Col. Mornement and the officers for providing the prizes.

It is proposed to have an inter-regimental team race for men of the various regiments stationed in the district. Particulars will be announced later.

song we knew — "It's a long way to Tipperary", "Pack up your troubles in your old kit bag and smile, smile, smile" and kept it up until we fell out for a rest at the roadside. What peaceful roads they were with never a motor car to be seen.

We all had good repertoires and even made up a song which we sang whenever our Provost Sergeant accompanied us. He was a plump and happy avuncular type of bachelor who was with J & J Colman Ltd. before he enlisted. He would smirk to himself and loop quickly past us when he heard this refrain:-

"There is a happy land, far, far, away,
Where mustard jolters work, three times a day,
Oh, you should see them run
When they see old father Bunn
Up and down the stairs they run
Three times a day."

Now you know his name.

It was not without good reason we infantrymen in the Great War were dubbed the PBI (Poor Bloody Infantry!) for the load we had to carry was heavy. Overcoats and ground sheets had to be packed in the valise strapped on our backs and the valises had to look neat in appearance or our inspecting officer would have had something to say about it. In this respect our officers really set us a good example in the perfect box-like shape of their valises which, somehow, we could never emulate. One afternoon, when we had fallen out for a rest on the grassy side of a country lane in Suffolk, we found out the reason why. A young officer left his equipment in the charge of his batman and was sitting a little way off with other officers when the batman mischievously unstrapped the perfect shaped valise and showed us there was nothing inside except a made-up cardboard box. We were roaring with laughter when the officer came on the scene, and he could do nothing else but join in.

We treated that as a good joke but took a dim view of our Company Commander when he accompanied us one day riding a spirited horse. We thought he needed the exercise more than we did and we grumbled amongst ourselves about his lack of sportsmanship in riding on horseback and looking very aloof as we foot-slogged in full marching order. The horse seemed more disturbed than we were, and it suddenly took into its head to rear up on its hind legs, doing its best to unhorse his rider and then charging down the country lane with the Company Commander trying desperately to bring it under control. They both disappeared from our view and that was the last time we saw him on a horse. We reckoned it served him right and we were not the least bit sympathetic.

There was little entertainment in Lowestoft for the troops and it was decided to re-open the Theatre for one night only and if it was well patronised to keep it going. Every soldier was asked to support it and to bring a friend. I invited the daughter of a jeweller to share two seats with me in the circle. The theatre was packed and as we ate chocolates during the first act, I screwed up the paper wrappers and put them on the padded shelf in front of me. When the lights went up at the interval, I flicked some into the stalls below and when I looked over the balcony, I saw my old-timer Sergeant Major looking up at me with a fierce expression on his face. I had flicked a wrapper on to his bald head.

One morning soon afterwards he appeared on the Promenade, for the first time ever, just as we were due to fall in for the early morning physical jerks. They were always held outside my billet which was very handy for me as I could watch from my window and when I saw the others starting to 'fall in' I could rush out and take my place before the Sergeant called the platoon to "attention".

This particular morning the Sergeant speeded up the operation when he saw the Sergeant Major approaching and I was a second too late. On the following Saturday morning the Sergeant Major peremptorily ordered me before the Orderly Officer.

I stood in front of the officer, who was seated at a table, and was not the least bit concerned as I felt the offence was trivial, when suddenly the Sergeant Major yelled out "TAKE YOUR CAP OFF" and snatched it off my head. Anger flared up inside me at this indignity, but outwardly I was cool as I explained my version of the 'charge' to the young officer. I felt he thought the old soldier had overstepped the mark as he told me in a pleasant tone not to be late again and dismissed me. I looked into the face of the Sergeant Major as I left the room. He was livid.

I never fell foul of him again as it was not long before the 2/4th Norfolk Regiment was split up as many of its members volunteered for Imperial Service overseas. I had no desire to leave the comforts of my billet at the Grand View nor to leave Lowestoft and deprive my family of the pleasure of visiting at weekends, so I decided to stay with the battalion and accept what fate had in store for me.

In September 1915 our wonderful stay in Lowestoft came to an end when we were ordered to Bawdsey, in Suffolk, a move that has been recorded by Lieutenant Colonel Edward Mornement, T.D., our Commanding Officer, in the following terms:

"…having completed the defences of Lowestoft, the battalion which, after the 2/4th was split up, was called the 61st Provincial battalion, moved to the Bawdsey — Hollesley — Orford coast defence section covering the northern defences of Harwich and Felixstowe where extensive fortifications were constructed. The Headquarters of the battalion were at Bawdsey Manor."

We detrained at Woodbridge station and marched the ten or more miles to Bawdsey. We had been trained to march but not to sleep on the stone floors of the stables of Bawdsey Manor. They were hard in more senses than one after the feather beds we had slept on for nearly two years and the army cooking was not too exciting after the splendid meals supplied by our billet ladies at Peterborough and Lowestoft. It was a complete contrast particularly in the evenings when there was nothing to do but sit in the stables or the one pub in the village. I have a most vivid recollection of standing on guard for two hours on top of a lonely cliff in the early hours of the morning. It was an eerie and unforgettable experience listening to all sorts of animal squeaks and rustlings in the long grass with everything in pitch darkness all around me. I was thankful when I was relieved.

On one occasion I came across the shirtless body of a tattooed seaman who had been washed up on the private beach of Bawdsey Manor. It was the first dead person I had seen and was a grim reminder of the perils of the sea in wartime.

After the disappointment of missing the opportunity of being transferred to Divisional Headquarters in Norwich and especially of being billeted at my home I made a point of reading Battalion Orders almost as soon as they were posted up each Monday morning and was interested to read that a shorthand clerk was required at Brigade Headquarters. I applied for the post and within a fortnight of arriving at Bawdsey, I was on my way to Saxmundham, where I was found a billet with a corn and coal merchant and his homely family who received seventeen shillings and six pence a week for my board and lodgings.

I was 'in clover' again with a small office to myself in a house on Fairfield Road where I worked from 9 to 5 o'clock as shorthand clerk to the Brigade Captain. I might as well have been a civilian, there were no drills or parades. Life in the small country town took some getting used to by a city dweller like myself, everybody knew everything about everybody else and the gossip had to be heard to be believed.

I found a letter amongst my sister Rosie's possession after she died which she had treasured for over forty years. I had sent it to my family on October 13th 1915, which was my nineteenth birthday, thanking them for the presents which they had sent me. Chocolate from father, gloves and handkerchiefs from mother, a pipe from sister Rosie, cigarettes from brother Reg and a bicycle tube from sister May. The bicycle tube would be useful for the old 'grid' I had bought for £1 and rode around the country lanes at lunch time. That was how lucky I was and how I amused myself while the soldiers of my battalion were drilling, marching and building defences in isolated areas around Bawdsey, Hollesley Bay and Shingle Street. I referred in the letter to the sad news of heavy casualties on the western front and was very glad to hear the Zeppelins had again been unable

Brother Reg and the Author in uniform.

to find Norwich. This was because the city lies in a hollow and black-out restrictions were strictly enforced, not like the slack conditions in Saxmundham, which I discovered when I went for a walk through the darkened street. The street lamps had been extinguished but flashing lights from hand torches nearly blinded me, and an old parson carried a bright acetylene lamp all the way down the street.

There was nothing a soldier could do in the evenings and the inevitable happened, I thought she was the most attractive girl in the small town and soon I was a regular visitor to her house.

She was the daughter of an officer in the Royal Marines Regiment which happened to be in Antwerp when the Germans overran the whole of Belgium two days before the commencement of the war on August 14th 1914. The rank and file were interned in Holland and the officers, including her father, were placed on parole and remained in Antwerp until the end of the war.

She had a nice soprano voice and was in demand at the church and at concerts. I felt proud when I escorted her to one of the concerts which the 1/6th Suffolk Cyclists arranged every Saturday night on the Layers. She had been invited to sing, and I sat in the front row of the large army hut which was packed with troops and civilians listening to her rendering of 'Roses in Picardy' and singing a duet with the Battalion's star baritone. Little did I realise I would be escorting a different soprano to concerts ten years later, but that is another story.

At the end of six months at Brigade Headquarters a fateful letter arrived, ordering me back to my battalion to join a draft for overseas and 'the party was over' for me.

My Staff Captain, a regular army officer, thoughtfully gave me an unsolicited letter which turned out to be the most important and crucial document I have ever received in my life. It undoubtedly saved me from being killed or wounded in action, like so many of the thousand young soldiers who crossed over to France with me in a crowded troopship a few weeks later and for this reason I have decided to include a copy:

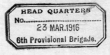
The bearer, No. 3549, L/Corpl. F. G. G. Cobb,
4th. Battalion, Norfolk Regiment, (attached
61st. Provisional Battalion) has been employed
as a clerk in the Brigade Office for the past
six months.

He is intelligent, conscientious and hard
working, and a proficient shorthand writer and
typist, and he has at all times carried out his
duties with entire satisfaction.

Having accepted the Imperial Service obligation
he leaves here to join a draft of the 61st. Provisional
Battalion for service overseas.

SAXMUNDHAM.
23. 3. 1916.

W. A. Ward

Captain.
Staff Captain.
6th. Provisional Brigade.

I said goodbye to my friends in Saxmundham, went off by train to Woodbridge and walked the ten miles to Bawdsey Manor in Suffolk, where I re-joined my battalion. Early the next morning a contingent of about twelve soldiers, including myself, were seen off by Captain W.C.C. Gaymer, whose personality and cheerfulness was a tonic and just what we needed as we were off to Salisbury Plain to join the 2/7th Worcesters which were under orders to leave for the fighting in France three weeks later.

I can only recollect two of my companions, Corporal West who hailed from Runton and Lance Corporal Gathergood who lived in St. Leonards Road, Norwich. The back yard of his home adjoined the 'chicken's run' at Norwich City's old football ground, 'The Nest'. I shall mention them both again later.

We arrived at Kandahar Barracks, Tidworth, late in the afternoon where we were assigned to different companies. I saw no more of the others after I had been escorted by a

Corporal of the 2/7th Worcester Regiment to a first-floor barrack room. He showed me what was to be my home for the time I would be on Salisbury Plain. It was a straw palliasse lying on bare boards, a locker, one of a long line in an uninviting room void of other furniture except a long table and some forms where soldiers ate their meals, wrote letters and played cards.

How different I felt then to the other occasions I had stepped into fresh billets during my eighteen months army service. There was the modest but homely terraced house in Peterborough, the boarding houses with sea views, comfortable lounges, feather beds and home cooking at Lowestoft and the friendly home of the coal and corn merchant at Saxmundham.

"Don't leave anything lying about or it will be pinched," warned the Corporal whose palliasse I had taken over and there was I, on my first evening in the barracks, completely cut off from the rest of the Norfolk lads. There was nowhere to go as the barracks and muddy plain were in complete darkness and I sat on my palliasse the whole of the evening with the Corporal's warning in my ears, watching the boisterous antics, and listening to the swearing of thirty or more young Worcestershire lads who took not the slightest notice of me, the only NCO present. I realised that I was in charge of the barrack room and felt alone and very much a stranger. It was no better the next morning when I washed and shaved in an ablution room instead of in a comfortable billet, took my dixie can to the army kitchen, and lined up for my breakfast which I ate at the long table in the barrack room in the company of two rows of hungry soldiers.

On parade that morning I found I was one of four Lance Corporals in my platoon in charge of a section of eight men. The Platoon Sergeant did not know I had not been on parade for six months, that I had never drilled anybody in my life, and that the unpaid stripe I was wearing on my arm had been given to me in the Brigade Office to raise me above the rank of the Orderly.

I must have disguised my shortcomings quite well as it was not long before he told me that, on his recommendation,

My "UNPAID" First Stripe

my rank had been substantiated and I would receive an extra sixpence a day.

There was an incident in the barrack room on the first evening that disturbed me very much although I soon found that sentiment had no place when a battalion was on battle training and its officers and NCOs had been instructed to enforce the strictest discipline as an integral part of the preparations for the fighting in France. The success of a battle could depend on the discipline of those taking part and where 'conduct to the prejudice of good order and military discipline', the most common offence in the army, was punished more severely than in England. The death sentence could be imposed and carried out for desertion, cowardice and other serious offences.

We were under the command of the 61st Infantry Division that had been ordered to embark for France three weeks later. In the barrack room several young lads were playing Nap at the table directly in front of me and they might just as well have been foreigners because I could not understand a word of their broad dialect. As the evening wore on they became more excitedly engrossed in their gambling as they won or lost and suddenly the youngest and noisiest of the bunch jumped to his feet with an oath, threw his cards on the table and rushed off as if he was being chased by a bull. He had been given 14 days C.B. for insubordination to his Platoon Sergeant and in the excitement of the game had gone past the time he should have reported to the guard room. He was five minutes late and was brought before the Commanding Officer the next day and sentenced to 14 days in the 'Glass House' on the Isle of Wight. When he came back, he was a changed lad, subdued and broken in spirit. He had been beaten, humiliated and subjected to all kinds of inhuman treatment and vowed he would never again do anything that would get him into trouble particularly so far as the Platoon Sergeant was concerned. The lad told me he never imagined the Sergeant would have taken such a serious view of the remarks he made to him as they had been brought up together in the same street and the Sergeant, who was several years older, even called on the boy's parents to say goodbye, promising them he would look after their son.

We finished our rigorous training with a three-day forced march across Salisbury Plain in full battle order. We carried everything we possessed in the packs on our backs a rifle, bayonet, entrenching tool, 100 rounds of ammunition in a bandoleer slung across the chest and over the shoulder, blanket, ground sheet, the lot. I am sure none of the rank and file will ever forget those three days.

The first night we slept in open fields and in the middle of the night the heavens opened. It rained in torrents for hours and we were soaked to the skin. The next morning the merciful sun shone on us as we marched, marched and marched. Steam rose upwards from our sodden uniforms and we could see it rising in clouds above the bobbing heads of the long line of troops in front of us who were ribboning their way across the bleak and muddy Plain. I often recalled that experience in the Second World War when I saw infantrymen being transported here and there in army lorries, the 'lucky beggars'.

One would be wrong to imagine our divisional commander was so impressed with our endurance that he went amongst his troops praising and encouraging them like Montgomery did in the desert. Our Major General decided to sustain our tired bodies by changing our diet. He put the whole of the 18,000 soldiers on iron rations and instead of bread ration we were issued with two dog biscuits for the day's consumption. They were too hard to eat or even soak in our tea. The name iron ration was very appropriate. I sent mine home as a memento with the inscription written on them "The army needs you and this is how it feeds you". We had bully beef stew at midday. It was greasy and horrible and our tea at teatime was boiled in the same dixies which had not been cleaned. It was awful to look at and to drink.

On the march strict orders were issued that no soldier must fall out and if he happened to be unable to march, he was to be left behind on Salisbury Plain to find his own way back to barracks. No wonder rumour had it that eleven died in these three days and the Divisional Commander had been reprimanded for driving his troops too hard. It was impossible to find out how the rumour came to be spread or if there was really any truth in it, but I was convinced from my experience that there could have been some truth in it. When we were dismissed on the barracks square on the evening of the third day, I just slumped to the ground, too exhausted to take off my heavy pack, and it was at least half an hour before my tired legs could carry me and my heavy pack and rifle up the stairs to our first floor barrack room. I have never felt so tired in all my life and the next morning I had to go on sick parade with sprained leg muscles. I was given 'light' duty but before finding out what it would entail, I decided to offer my suggestions to my Commanding Officer by writing him a letter enclosing with it a copy of the Brigade Staff Captain's testimonial and suggesting I could purposefully perform my light duties in the Battalion orderly room. My suggestion found favour and I busied myself for a fortnight with clerical duties and was recalled to my platoon for intensive infantry training a few days before embarkation to France. Looking back, I'm sure it was my sixth sense and my destiny that guided my pen to write that letter which was the cause of eventually changing the pattern of my whole life.

We had our last leave to say goodbye to our loved ones before we left for France and on our return to barracks, we suffered the crowning indignity of having our hair shorn as close to the skin as possible with number one clippers. Our heads looked like big eggs and we were glad our families and friends could not see us. There were thousands of 'skinheads' on Salisbury Plain at that time and I can assure you they were kept completely under control.

There was one Lance Corporal who was very disturbed as the day of embarkation drew near. He locked himself in an ablution room in the barracks opposite. We could see inside from our windows and we saw him nailing up the door from the inside, then marching up and down between rows of washbasins with his rifle and fixed bayonet sloped on his shoulder. When someone banged on the door from the other side he would stop and bring his rifle to the 'on guard' position. After a while military police arrived and broke down the door and an army doctor appeared in the opening, gesticulating, as if urging the soldier to put down his rifle.

We could not hear the dialogue but saw the soldier remain at 'the ready' and lunge forward several times as if preparing himself to bayonet anyone who dared approach him, then as if he had been given an order to 'slope arms, quick march' he brought the rifle to his shoulder and marched off in military style, through the doorway and out of sight followed by the doctor and the MPs. Some of the lads from Worcestershire who knew him well reckoned he was trying to work his ticket or putting on an act to evade overseas service in the trenches but, whatever prompted his unusual behaviour, he was not on the troopship that took us over to France and I never ever heard of him again.

Chapter 5 — World War 1 France, May 1916–October 1917

We crossed the English Channel from Southampton to Le Havre one dark night in May 1916, or at least we thought we had. We were packed in the hold of a troopship like sardines in a tin. We tried to sleep but halfway across the channel there was a sharp impact, the ship shuddered violently as if in a collision and we were thrown on top of each other. The Sergeant Major yelled to us to remain where we were. We obeyed his command, there was no panic and, as nothing further happened, we settled down again. The next morning the engine stopped, and we went on deck to take our first look at France. To our surprise we were back in Southampton Water and the ship had a large dent in her bows. We disembarked and spent the whole day in sheds on the docks. At nightfall we were off again in another troopship and landed at Le Havre the next morning.

As far as the men around me were concerned it seemed that our short stay in Le Havre was without interest but for me it was the turning point of my life. I have often felt my happy existence had been ordained but never as strongly as the morning we paraded at the camp awaiting the command to march to the railway station where we were to entrain for the journey to our first turn of duty in the trenches. I looked at the soldiers in my platoon and noticed that the faces of those rugged young Worcestershire lads were uncharacteristically pensive.

They, like me, were facing up to the future, wondering what destiny had in store for them at the end of the journey. As one of them had said "If a bullet has my name on it there is nothing I can do about it." All at once it seemed to me, I had received a message, I looked again at those soldiers and my innermost thoughts seem to be saying "I will not be with them all much longer". That conviction remained with me during my first week in the trenches.

We had a long march from our rest billets to the trenches at dusk about a week after we had landed in France and were received in the glare of Very Lights by an amazing collection of soldiers, all of them around about five feet tall. We had to spend the next week in the trenches under instruction from a bantam battalion.

I envied them their lack of height especially when walking with them in the communication trenches. They could walk upright without fear of a sniper bullet and like the Emperor Napoleon, who was only five feet two inches in height, and in whose adopted country they were fighting, they too were 'strong, sensible and courageous'.

This was the period of the Great War when communications from France read *"all quiet on the Western Front"*. I remember, in particular, the intensity of the German machine-gun fire. They would open up at dusk, as if the guns were operated by a time switch and bullets would literally clip the top of the parapet. It was definitely the case of keeping your head down. I could see paths through the mud made with unopened bully beef tins and huge rats, nearly as big as cats, silhouetted in the moonlight as they ran along the tops of the trenches.

I was in the dugout one afternoon with a bantam sergeant watching rats emerge at intervals from a hole in the earth wall. They would drop from the hole to the ground and scurry out through an opening in the opposite side of the dug-out. The sergeant invited me to watch. He stood in front of the hole with a bayonet in his hand and when the next rat was halfway to the ground, he pierced it with his bayonet and held it aloft in triumph. I was shocked and wondered if the war would make me as callous when I had been in France as long as he had; which he told me was three months. We came out of the trenches and spent the next week 'resting' at an evacuated farmstead. The countryside was desolate and forbidding. Apart from a game of football, which I enjoyed, the week was uneventful.

An amusing thing happened on the first night. A few NCOs, including myself, decided to find a more cosy place to sleep other than the huge barn which was being allocated to the men of my company. We found a small outbuilding where there was just room on the stone floor to spread a ground sheet and blanket. One of the party saw, above his bed, an opening in the ceiling which had been blocked up with straw. He jumped up several times and pulled down sufficient straw to make himself a comfortable mattress and congratulated himself loudly for our special benefit.

While we slept, the rats on the floor above us started their nightly gambolling and one of them fell through the hole left in the ceiling after the straw had been removed. We were wakened by a heavy thud and a yell. The thud was the sound of the heavy impact of a rat, when it dropped on the previously exultant soldier who was sleeping contentedly directly under the hole. He jumped up with a startled yell, and we all chuckled and shouted in turn as we ducked our heads under our blankets and felt the rat running around the room over our bodies. All was in darkness in the tiny outhouse except for a hole in the bottom of the door through which we could see the moonlight outside. The rat saw the hole too and, to our relief, bolted through it. After several more rats had fallen and scurried over us and out into the moonlit yard we went to sleep. I realised after that experience why there is a hole at the bottom of farm building doors.

The day arrived when we were under orders to take over full duties in the trenches for the first time. The changeover would take place at dusk and we were not looking forward to it. We were somewhere near Neuve Chappelle on a beautiful June morning in 1916 when Corporal West, a military policeman, told me that I was wanted at the Orderly Room. When I got there, I was instructed to proceed immediately to the headquarters of the XI Army Corps at Hinges for duty as a clerk. I went back to my platoon to collect my rifle and all my possessions and West, who hailed from West Runton, was curious to know why I had been sent for. When I told him, he ejaculated, "The biggest fools (he pronounced it "fewls" in broad Norfolk) get the best of luck". As I walked the ten miles to Hinges, I pondered over West's remark and dismissed the first part after a little self-analysis. Then I began to wonder if it really was luck that I had been selected from eighteen thousand soldiers for that position, and was marching from the dangers and tribulations of trench warfare to the comparative safety and comfort of the head-quarters of an Army Corps; or had it anything to do with that strange feeling that first possessed me at Le Havre and ever since. Could it be that some mysterious power was shaping my destiny? I learnt later that I had taken the place of a soldier who was sent back to a fighting unit when the 61st division replaced his division in the XI Corps, and I could expect to be sent back to my Battalion when the 61st division moved to another command in four to five months' time.

I reported for duty at the DAA & QMG's office which was on the ground floor of a château. Every other room in the château was occupied, either as offices, bedrooms or an officers mess, by a fabulous collection of regular army staff officers of every rank from Lieutenant-General to his aides-de-camp who were at that time Lieutenant Robertson, whose father rose from the ranks to become Field Marshal Sir William Robertson and to eventually succeed Lord Kitchener as Military Adviser to the British government, and Second Lieutenant Bairnsfather, who was a younger brother of the famous cartoonist, Bruce Bairnsfather, the creator of Old Bill, young Bart and the "Better 'Ole".

At the back of the chateau were army huts that housed the Intelligence, Maps, Signals, Ordinance, RAMC, Artillery and other services that constitute an Army Corp Establishment.

I felt strange the first few days and was thankful to be able to sit and type the letters that had accumulated awaiting my arrival. It was so different. Nobody had closely cropped hair like mine; not that anybody took any notice as far as I could see. I found out later I was wrong about this as one morning the Corps Padre, a major, stopped me and smilingly said "I like the Russo-Grecian style of your hair, I wish I could get mine to grow like it."

I had to check myself from being regimental as I had been trained to be with the Worcesters, although it was really out of character for me, and I very soon settled down to work with some of the nicest chaps I had ever known.

They had all enlisted at the commencement of the war as clerks in the Army Service Corps and they had done no barrack square-bashing or been subject to any real army discipline. They attended no parades of any kind and it was just like working in the office I left at Norwich Thorpe station where I had been shorthand clerk to the District Goods Manager.

These clerks knew more about the army than I did when they enlisted in 1914. The only place I had heard of was the Drill Hall, Chapel Field Road, Norwich, where I presented myself one morning, without, I am ashamed to say, telling my parents beforehand. I also, very impetuously, ignored an ultimatum issued by the General Manager of the Great Eastern Railway that no more clerks will be released for army service and ran the risk of being dismissed from the railway for disobeying orders. A sergeant named R.H. Mottram put my name in his notebook and assigned me to "B" company, known as the Business Company of the 2/4th Royal Norfolk Regiment.

Little did I imagine that sergeant would become Lord Mayor of Norwich and a famous author who, when he reached the ripe old age of 87 years, would present to the city of Norwich 69 holograph manuscripts and 21 other publications including "The Spanish Farm" which won the Hawthorden prize in 1924. Unlike my newfound friends at XI Corps, I think I can claim to have arrived at the Château by a harder route, but what a fine experience it had been for me at nineteen years of age.

We often saw Sir Richard Haking, the Corps Commander, walking past our office window with an aide-de-camp in attendance. He looked every inch a General and a gentleman. His handsome, and to my young mind, fairly elderly face was relaxed and kindly. He must have inspired complete confidence in all the officers under his command. His well-groomed appearance was emulated by all his regular army staff officers who were at all times immaculate in their well-tailored uniforms resplendent with decoration ribbons, red tabs and hat bands and the gold insignia of the rank.

Staff cars and dispatch riders came and departed all day long and the military activity around the château sharply contrasted with the peacefulness of the secluded grounds. Some way removed from the château was the tiny village which was just a collection of peasant cottages on either side of a country road where all was tranquil. By the grace of God, the village had not yet experienced the ravages of war.

There was no apparent social life except in the estaminet where some of the elderly locals forgathered in the evenings. On Sundays the whole village would "*s'endimancher*" or as we English take much longer to say, they would "put on their Sunday clothes" and go to church; the old men in black suits and the women in long black crêpe dresses. The white confirmation frocks of young girls provided a pleasant contrast to the sombre clothing of their elders and seemed to symbolise continuity of life in the village.

The menfolk of military age were away fighting for their country and those left behind went quietly about their daily tasks. To tell the truth, I cannot say what their daily tasks were except those of one French family of humble 'paysans' who lived in a spotlessly clean cottage. There was grandfather who was getting on for eighty years of age; his married daughter whom we respectfully called Madame and her two children, a girl of fourteen and a boy of twelve. I was taken to that cottage for my first meal after my arrival at the château. It was about five minutes' walk away and when I entered the neat and tidy room I saw a shining cooking stove with the customary coffee pot standing on top. There were some pleasant looking, young non-commissioned officers having tea at a table laid for eight persons. I realised the era of the dog biscuits and army stew had passed me by, temporarily at any rate, and I could put away my Dixie can and mug. The mess had been in existence for some time and I was pleased to have been invited to become a member. Lance Corporal Riley, a regular army clerk with the Assistant Director of Medical Services, collected our rations from Army Stores every morning and took them to Madame. She prepared, cooked and served meals at her cottage, and for that excellent service we paid her five francs every week and a little more for anything extra she had to provide. A franc was worth ten pence and twenty-four francs went to a £1 sterling. We could make purchases with either pennies or ten centimes which were of the same value.

Madame used to completely immerse our meat ration in boiling fat which was in a large pot on the top of the cooking stove. There was no comparison between meat cooked that way and the notoriously tough 'horse' served by Army cooks from their field kitchens. I can honestly say we never had a tough piece of meat. The sudden immersion into the boiling fat sealed the juices inside the meat, the taste was delicious and so was the soup that Madame never failed to serve first. I thought of the folks at home making do with their meagre rations and counted my blessings.

Our Quartermaster Sergeant was a regular army soldier. Mild-mannered, patient and thoughtful, he lived for his work. He needed only two and a half hours sleep at night and spent every evening at his desk. We worked with him most nights as there was nothing else to do. If we had a rush of work, we often stayed until midnight and I wondered what I would have said if I'd been asked to do that when I was working for the Great Eastern Railway.

My zeal and industry seemed to be taken for granted by higher authority and there was no reason why it should not have been because the job had to be done. I had no idea at all that my future on XI Corps was being discussed. I knew my Division was under orders to move to another Corps and I expected any day to be sent back to my battalion. There was no vacancy on the Establishment for another clerk, and even if there had been, an Army Service Corps clerk would have been sent from Base to fill it. I made no approach to any officer or senior NCO in an effort to stay on at Corps Headquarters because it seemed so futile, bearing in mind what happened to my predecessors. I had become a fatalist like many of the soldiers serving in France.

One thing was certain, I would never re-join the 2/7th Worcesters, as such, because that Battalion and the 2/8th

Worcesters, who fought side-by-side, had such heavy casualties during the five months I had been away from them that it had been necessary to regroup them into one single Battalion which was named the 2/8th Worcesters.

Corporal West had told me when I left the 2/7th that the biggest fools get the best of luck. It was, of course, 'sour grapes' and I wonder what he would have said if he had known I would not be returning. I prefer to think it was Destiny again shaping my future.

It happened like this, the ADMS, a Major General, was getting old and had no need of the horse and groom to which he was entitled by virtue of rank and office. This left a vacancy on the Establishment for a groom, and my superior officers requested the Camp Commandant to insert my name in the vacant space. Thus, on paper, I became a groom but continued to absorb myself in most interesting clerical duties until I was demobilised more than two years later.

When the 61st division moved to the Somme the last link was broken and I read no more reports of its operations. There had often been sad moments when familiar names appeared in the casualty lists and there were many others whose passing distressed me. One in particular was Captain T.A.K. Cubitt ('Tak' to his friends). He was well known to readers of the *Eastern Daily Press* for articles published over his initials and his future seemed assured. Since we were together in the 2/4th Norfolk, he had written most interesting letters to me, and I went to see him when his battalion was 'resting' near Hinges. He was killed when leading an attack on the enemy, and his colleagues told me later, he could have assigned the mission to his sergeant, but never asked anybody to do anything he thought he should do himself. He was an extremely popular officer and his loss was keenly felt by the men of his Company.

He was awarded the Military Cross.

Recommendations for awards of decorations for bravery in the field came in from time to time from the several Divisions in the Corps and, after review by the Corps Commander, were passed on to the Headquarters of the First Army. I watched with great personal interest a recommendation from Officer Commanding 2/8th Worcester Regiment that the Victoria Cross should be awarded to Sergeant Gathergood, for consistent bravery under heavy enemy fire in attempting to rescue, on several occasions, wounded soldiers lying in 'no man's land'. The Brigade Commander had endorsed the recommendation. This was the Gathergood who left Bawdsey Manor with me eight or nine months previous. It was very bad luck for him that just before the citation reached Division Headquarters an edict had been issued by Sir Douglas Haig, who had just succeeded Lord French as Commander-in-Chief of the BE Force, that the Victoria Cross would not be awarded in future for acts of bravery in saving, or attempting to save, the lives of wounded soldiers because of the heavy casualties to would-be rescuers.

This was at the time of the battle of the Somme. There had been heavy attacks and counter-attacks by the Germans and although the positions remained practically unaltered the tremendous losses in manpower had seriously reduced the fighting strength of the British Army. It was for this reason the edict had been issued.

The divisional commander had, perforce, to amend the recommendation to state "The Distinguished Conduct Medal" and that decoration was conferred on Sergeant Gathergood.

I feel sure he knew nothing of the great honour that would have been bestowed on him, if his acts of bravery had taken place earlier, or at the battle of the Somme a little later. I had no opportunity of telling him. I heard that he joined the special police in Ireland known as the 'Black and Tans' soon after he was demobilised and that he died not many years later. One would never have imagined him a Sergeant in the frontline. He used to sit, as the driver, high up on one of the two colossal army lorries the 2/4th Norfolk's had at Lowestoft in 1915. He looked so diminutive from ground level and could not have been more than eighteen years of age.

The Battle of the Somme also seriously depleted the officer strength of the British Expeditionary Force and OC battalions were urgently requested to seek out and recommend men suitable for commissioned rank. Those selected were, in the main, sergeants and non-commissioned officers of lower rank with good educations and social backgrounds. They arrived at Corps Headquarters in increasing numbers to be interviewed by Sir Richard Haking who recorded on their commission forms his observations as to their suitability for commissioned rank.

Those forms passed through my hands. I remember in particular a young Sergeant Major who the Corps Commander had singled out for special mention. He was of humble birth, the son of a farm labourer. He went to the village school and afterwards worked for the local horticulturalist doing menial tasks, but since joining the army he had proved himself to be an excellent soldier, and leader of men, and was highly praised and recommended by his Commanding Officer. The Corps Commander endorsed the recommendations of the Brigade and Division Commander. He was more impressed with the military ability of that young countryman than the academic qualifications of the other candidates he had interviewed and added a rider that Commanding Officers should seek out 'yeoman soldiers' as candidates for commissions as they will make excellent wartime officers. It struck me forcibly that the distinguished General had driven a wedge in the old traditional method of selecting officers from the 'upper strata' and the professions.

As time passed, I began to specialise in Courts Martial under a Corps Courts Martial Officer, which was a new post created by the Judge Advocate General. The work involved, inter alia, careful scrutiny of all Courts Martial Proceedings, to ensure that the charge and the recorded evidence conformed to the Manual of Military Law and the King's Regulations, both of which I got to know very well. It was very important, especially to the accused soldier who had been tried by Court Martial, that the scrutiny should be thorough.

Not infrequently an irregularity was found, and the sentence quashed on a point of law. I can quote a case to illustrate this which you are most likely to find hard to believe, but I can assure you, even though I too am relying on my memory, the facts are substantially correct.

A Court Martial was convened by a Division not then in the XI Corps, and the accused soldier was given a sentence of nine years penal servitude. The Court Martial proceedings reached the Judge Advocate General at GHQ who quashed the sentence because the evidence recorded at the trial had been written on both sides of the foolscap sheets of paper which was contrary to military law. The soldier got off scot free.

It was at GHQ that the final decision was made as to whether the sentences of death should be confirmed or commuted to prison sentences. If confirmed the Proceedings of Court Martial were returned to the Convening Officer with the simple signature of "D. Haig" on the last page. If Sir Douglas Haig, Commander in Chief had appended his signature then at a specified time and day the execution of the sentence would be carried out in a private place. The condemned man would be shot by twelve soldiers chosen at random from another regiment, with a witness from his own regiment, usually the Adjutant, in attendance. The death would be recorded as a casualty on active service.

A Court Martial for other ranks consisted of a President of the Court, usually a Major, with the Captain and a Lieutenant. There was always a Prosecutor, the Adjutant of the accused's battalion, an officer was selected to act as the 'prisoner's friend' and the whole of the proceedings at the trial carefully written out in longhand. The verdict was also recorded and the Court Martial Proceedings, as they were called, eventually arrived on my desk for the action I have already described.

In all cases involving serious crimes where the death sentence or extremely heavy prison sentences had been imposed by a Court Martial it was my duty to prepare a precis of the evidence for the Corps Commander so that he did not have to wade through the whole of the written evidence. I would remove the précis before sending the Proceedings to the 1st Army Headquarters as they were of no more value to the XI Corps than an office chit but to me, they were something special and personal, the first literary achievements in my young life.

I felt like a reporter reading his first published article and the work became more interesting and absorbing as my experience grew. I kept them all for their human interest and also, I must confess, because I hated to destroy what I had so diligently prepared to my own satisfaction.

I fully intended to bring them home with me when I was demobilised but, at the last minute, I had fears that they might be discovered when I passed through the demobilisation centre and my civilian life put in temporary jeopardy, so I burnt them.

There were thirty one death sentences in the collection, and they revealed grim stories of men whose mental and emotional stability had been disturbed beyond human limit by the tragic and awful things they had seen and endured in that bloody fighting area. I am glad now I destroyed them, although in the proper hands they would have provided excellent material for a dramatic war story. It has been said that every person has at least one good story inside him or her, who knows, I might have produced a bestseller.

It is gratifying to remember that each individual case was very carefully and sympathetically considered by the highest authority, all extenuating circumstances taken into account, and that the majority of the death sentences were commuted to varying periods of penal servitude.

For the record 3,080 death sentences were pronounced by British Courts Martial in the First World War but only 346 of the sentences were carried out. A few in the latter category had been sentenced to death twice. The majority had been tried for desertion while under orders to attack or in the face of the enemy.

I remember two Canadian soldiers being brought to trial for murder. It was early one morning when the landlord and his wife were asleep in their estaminet, which was on a lonely road. They were awakened by shouting and heavy banging on the street door. They opened their bedroom window and saw two drunken soldiers below who ordered the landlord to go downstairs and serve them with drink.

He refused and told them to go away, where upon they became more aggressive, kicking the door and shouting up abuse and obscenities which only stopped when they shot the unfortunate man dead at the side of his stricken wife. It was a most distressing case.

Later we began to get more leisure time from the office and turns of duty were arranged which gave us an afternoon, and sometimes a Sunday, off duty. I often strolled around the grounds of the château alone, except for my constant companion, a stray fox terrier, who used to perform such tricks as jumping over an outstretched stick as many times as I wished. He always slept at the foot of my bed and I got extremely fond of him. It was very disappointing when I had to leave him behind at Hinges about a year later.

Sergeant Parrott, Corporal Over and I walked into Bethune almost every week and enjoyed a cup of coffee and some delicious cakes at a baker's shop in the Grand Place. They only sold homemade bread and cakes, but we prevailed upon the baker's wife to serve us with coffee to help the cakes down. There was very little room in the shop for us and the customers and after a few visits we were invited to drink coffee in the living room where we enjoyed chatting with the homely baker, his wife and their three daughters. Two of the latter were like elder sisters to us and the youngest, Simone, who had not long left school, spoke perfect English and was so faultlessly naturally ladylike and composed that we felt a trifle awed in her presence. They all seemed to look forward to our visits.

In the summer of 1917, the XI Corps organised some sports in a field adjacent to the château for the special entertainment of the local populace. I asked the parents of Simone if we could take her to the sports and they readily agreed. I have forgotten how she got from Bethune to Hinges, but I imagine I walked the five miles to fetch her and took her back afterwards. It was a red letter day for Parrott, Over and myself. Simone had dressed herself in her Sunday best with a picture hat which suited her very well, and she stood out like a Paris model among the plainly dressed countryfolk. We could feel the admiring and surprised glances of the officers and the furtive looks of the villagers, but I'm sure that Simone was totally unaware of all that.

72

We talked about it for weeks and each of us would refer to her in conversation as "MY Simone" with special emphasis on the "MY".

That sports day outing was an isolated occasion and we had no further opportunity of inviting her out. There was a happy ending to the story. I heard from a source I have forgotten that little Sergeant Parrott, who in civilian life was with a local newspaper in Reading, married Simone after the war. It was a great surprise to me and a pleasant one.

The owner of the château moved out when the war started and left a fierce looking bewhiskered little Frenchman, the natives called 'Le gardien', to look after the house and grounds. He walked around the place every day with quick steps; a big black dog at his heels, and a big stick in his hand. If he saw anybody walking where he thought they should not be, he shouted and shook his stick at them until they kept to the paths. When we saw him coming, we would say to each other "Look out, here comes old fuzzy whiskers!" and managed to keep out of trouble. He need not have been so fussy as the Germans spoiled everything, except the tower.

One afternoon I was taking a solitary walk around the grounds with my dog when I saw the rare sight of a Frenchman of military age in civilian clothes. He must have been a soldier on leave out for an afternoon's sport because he appeared to be fishing in the lake. He had a long fishing rod and line and had baited the hook with short lengths of brightly coloured wool which he dangled in front of a big toad sitting in the water. The toad was attracted by the bright colour and snapped up the wool and the hook. The man then gave the rod a sudden jerk and swung it upwards and over his head which sent the toad flying through the air on the end of the line; screaming like a frightened pig until it struck the ground with a distinct thud. Then there was silence. What an unearthly noise those toads made and what a way to spend an afternoon!

The war was dragging on with no sign of an early ending. There had been many staff changes, there was a new DAA & QMG, a Staff Major Codrington, whose father was a well-

Jock Shepherd – From Sterling
"MY IDEAL SCOTSMAN"

known serving General. He was a tall, well-built, capable officer and a gentleman, as I was to find out later.

Lance Corporal Mumford who first escorted me to our Mess in the village became a close friend and I missed his company when he went to England for a commission in the Royal Naval Air Force which had just been formed. He sent me a photograph of himself in the navy-blue uniform that had been adopted for the new Force but he soon had to discard it when the Force lost its identity and was placed under the control of the Royal Flying Corps, whose officers and other ranks wore khaki uniforms.

Jock Shepherd, a handsome Scot from Stirling, took his place as my companion. He was the first Scotsman I had really known, and his generous nature was a revelation to me after having heard stories about Glasgow being deserted on flag days which erroneously labelled the Scotsman as a 'tightfisted' individual. As a wartime friend he made a great impression on me and inoculated me with a liking for Scottish people. I heard that after the war he had a job calling on farmers throughout Norfolk, many of whom turned out to be Scots.

When we met he was a Lance Corporal, next he was a Quartermaster Sergeant, and a month or two later, to my dismay, he left XI Corps Headquarters to take up a post as

Warrant Officer, Class I, Royal Ordinance Corps at First Army Headquarters.

There was a spate of promotions in the Corps offices among the Army Service Corps personnel (the 'Royal' had not been then added to the title) which I could not participate in as I was still on the strength of the Worcestershire Regiment and any promotion for me would have had to be authorised by the Commanding Officer, an unlikely eventuality, as it would have deprived a soldier fighting in the trenches of a well-deserved promotion. I was given the next best thing, once again, an extra unpaid stripe, which at least made me look like the other clerks. My army pay was one shilling and nine pence a day which included the princely sum of three pence a day infantry proficiency.

It was an eye opener to me when I learned one could have enlisted as a clerk in the ASC with the rank of a private, and get three shillings and six pence a day, which was the same rate of pay as an Infantry Sergeant in charge of a platoon of forty men who could be risking his life in the firing line.

I could not help feeling envious when my colleagues were handed three times as much as me on pay day for doing the same sort of work but it did not affect my morale or dampen my spirit. I well remember little Joe Davis, our meek and mild Welsh orderly, who was well past military age, coming up to me one morning when I was dressing and saying, "Oh Corporal, I do love to hear you singing first thing in the mornings." It is strange how we do things regularly day after day for years and it is only when someone draws attention to them, they assume great significance in your life. I realised I was the only soldier in the hut who sang in the mornings and I usually started off with the curtain raiser of the Goodman's Pierrots who gave performances every summer at the Nest, which was the football ground of Norwich City Football Club. The stage was erected on the playing pitch and the audiences sat in the grandstand.

I wonder if there are any alive who can remember the song:-

"Oh! We are the gay Pierrots
The Goodman's Gay Pierrots
We sing and jest, and do our best,
To drive away your woes,
Laughing, dancing, singing
Whilst we drive your cares away
Whilst — we drive your cares away."

I could not keep Norwich out of my thoughts for very long.
Every young soldier from Norwich I met on active service,
(and you could not fail to recognise them when they spoke)
suffered from nostalgia and enthused over 'dear old
Norridge'. We left our homes so early in life we knew little of
the finer attributes of the 'Fine City'. To us there was
Mousehold where we played football and did a spot of
courting at night. The 'chicken's run' was the name given to
Prince of Wales Road where literally hundreds of young
people of both sexes paraded the pavements every night, and
in increasing numbers on Saturday and Sunday nights.
Willmott's side was the shilling side, the pavement on the
other side, where Pike's Dairy was; we called the half-crown
side because it was always less crowded and favoured by the
more sedate strollers. The Castle Museum was high in popularity on Sunday afternoons as a rendezvous for youngsters
as admission was free.

We were proud of our cathedral and knew it was 315 feet
high and the golden cockerel on top of the spire was as big
as a small donkey, but few had been inside to admire the
lofty nave, the beautiful roof with its 328 bosses carved with
spiritual scenes, and the other fine examples of Norman
architecture. We thought of Pull's Ferry as the house where
the ferryman lives who would take you across the river in
his flat-bottomed boat if you tolled the bell and gave him a
penny. We did not realise the house was at one time an Inn
within the cathedral precincts and the medieval flintwork
Watergate used to span the mouth of a canal that was cut
from the river to within a few feet of the site of the Norwich
Cathedral, in order to facilitate the transport of stone for the
building of the Cathedral.

We would pass unnoticed medieval doorways which had the trademarks of City merchants carved on their lintels and we would not have given a second thought to the magnificent specimen of flintwork in the wall of the Guildhall, or to the smooth black flints of the Bridewell "so admirably squared and put together as scarcely to admit a knife edge between the joints". The drabness of Fishergate, for example, was never brightened by turning our minds back to the middle ages when fisherfolk landed their catches there and worshipped in the church of St. Edmund, where a piece of Saint Edmund's shirt was supposed to have been preserved. The church is now used as a warehouse, but you can still stand on the spot where St. Edmund stood, and gaze up at the half of his personal shield which is still in its original position in the roof.

We young soldiers would have been doubly proud of our city if we had known what the pioneers of the Norwich Publicity Association have, in the last two decades, so successfully brought to the notice of the people of Norwich and to the world in general. Soon after Major Ernest Felce was appointed its first secretary, he took me for a walk around the city to help me find material for an article about Norwich. What I was shown opened my eyes to the tremendous wealth of antiquarian treasures, and I have been interested ever since.

Our sleeping quarters at Hinges was a Nissen hut that was comfortably heated by a huge tortoise stove. As I lay on my mattress, I could see little field mice scampering about on a ledge a few feet away. They had found a haven from the severe winter's grip on their natural habitat, the flat, hedgeless fields outside, and were playing like happy kittens whilst we humans were killing and wounding each other because of the whim of power-crazed Kaiser Bill. My comrades were either sleeping or thinking, unaware of the presence of the mice and undisturbed by the croaking of the toads and the noise of mortars from the distant front line. Little Sergeant Parrott could have been weaving a web of charming hypothesis around his thoughts of Simone, the vivacious young girl hardly out of school, who used to join the family in chatting to us when we were having coffee at the baker's shop in Bethune. A hypothesis that eventually changed to blissful reality when he married her. Where else could Sergeant Riley's thoughts have been with a name like that but in his "dear 'ole Oireland". The young clerk who worked in the Corps Military Police could have been quietly thinking of home sweet home, but his heart would have beaten much faster if he had known then that on his ten days leave to Blighty, he would be proudly wearing the ribbon of the Belgian *Croix de Guerre* on his chest. It happened like this – the grateful Belgian Army had passed on to the Headquarters of the British Expeditionary Forces in France a number of medals for distribution to soldiers who had distinguished themselves in the Belgium theatre of war and one was allotted to XI Corps HQ. Our Camp Commandant asked for the names of those who had served in Belgium, and the young Corporal was the only one. He had been in Belgium two or three weeks before being posted to XI Corps!

I often thought of the lads in my battalion who were fighting in the trenches. I owed no allegiance to my Battalion nor did I form any sort of friendship with the men in my platoon. In the short time I was with them I had not got beyond the 'foreigner' stage, as they were all Worcester-shire boys, but I was truly concerned that I was enjoying freedom from danger. I had so many privileges denied to infantrymen, such as parades, drills, duty in the trenches and strict discipline. I asked myself many times whether or not I ought to be with my battalion. I knew only too well that my infantry experience, especially in the front line, was sadly lacking and I would now be hopeless as a non-commissioned officer.

I saw myself as no different to the able-bodied officers and NCOs on the Headquarters staff; they had no qualms as to where their duty lay and I reasoned that as I was faithfully discharging the duties I had been ordered to perform I would carry on and let fate decide my future. One of the first privileges I received after making this decision was leave of absence after only seven months in France. I spent ten wonderful days, including Christmas 1916, with my over-joyed family and with Herbert 'Bummy' Minors, one of my old chums, now a Sergeant, who by a lucky chance had leave from his unit, somewhere in England, for exactly the same period as myself. If I had not met him it would have been very dull in Norwich as all our acquaintances were in the Forces and there were men in khaki everywhere, and Military Policemen pacing the pavements in pairs. I was thankful for my good fortune in getting a leave pass so quickly and, at the same time, could not help feeling sorry for the Tommies who had been in France for such a long time with no immediate hope of getting home. I found out the real facts about this distressing situation when I got back to Hinges. The DAA. & QMG First Army asked Headquarters for the leave roster position in the three divisions under its command, suggesting it might be possible, while the military situation remained stalemate, to increase leave permits at battalion level, which would have the two-fold effect of reducing the length of time a soldier would have to wait before he went home on leave, and of boosting the morale of the troops. Statistics were obtained from the Divisions which showed quite a number had not had leave for nearly two years, and one 'old contemptible' had been in France for two and a half years, without leave. He was given a pass as soon as his Commanding Officer knew about it and as a result of the research the allotment of leaves was increased.

This small record of the war in France may seem common-place in print but imagine the emotions aroused in those men when they were handed their unexpected leave passes and how the hearts of their loved ones must have been lifted from the depths of despair when their soldier boy appeared on the threshold in his mud bespattered uniform and his rifle on his shoulder.

I was very lucky to be granted ten days leave on three occasions during my 2¾ years in France. I remember telling little Joe Davis, our Orderly, who I liked talking to because he seemed so lonely, how the last night of my leave turned out to be a sort of anti-climax to an otherwise extremely enjoyable ten days. My two sisters were working on 'muni-

79

tions' and their turn of duty finished at 10.00pm. They were allowed to leave off work at 8.00pm so they could spend the last two brief hours with me and see me off at Thorpe station. When they were about to leave work a terrific storm was raging, with thunder, lightning and torrential rain. My sisters, like many other girls of their age, had an inherent fear of lightning and I have recollections of them and my mother shutting themselves up in a cupboard at the height of an electric storm, but on this occasion their regard for me miraculously transcended their fears and they braved the lightning and the blinding rain for twenty minutes on their walk home from 'Munitions'. The storm had not abated when we walked to the station in the 'blackout'; sister May stepped off the pavement into a six inch puddle and then when we were walking along the 'blacked out' station platform, which was packed with sodden soldiers and their sweethearts, she turned to smile at a friend and walked into one of the iron stanchions that supported the roof. This brought tears to her eyes, but in spite of all that, they would not have missed seeing me off for worlds.

I told Joe Davis about that experience when I got back, and he reminded me of it on his return from leave some months later. "Oh Corporal" he said to me, his quiet Welsh voice tinged with sadness "I did envy you having someone to see you off at the station. When I got home, I found my wife had got a man lodger and, do you know, she made more fuss of him than she did me. When I was ready to come away, she was in the kitchen and I went in and said, "I'm off now."

All she said in reply was "I hope you are not going to make a fuss about it." Poor Joe's spirits were shattered, and he felt sadly alone and neglected when he sat in a train at Cardiff station and watched wives and other loved ones so emotionally saying goodbye to their departing soldier-boys.

Chapter 6 — World War 1
Italy, October 1917–January 1918

From the long winter of 1916 to October 1917 chroniclers of the Great War record the British attack at Arras, the capture of Vimy Ridge and 13,000 prisoners, the advance of the French on the Champagne front when many prisoners were taken and the German counterattacks which nullified the previous combined efforts of the Allies armies.

The sector of the XI Corps, still under the command of Sir Richard Haking, remained stalemate, the Germans holding the same positions as they did when they halted their first advance in the last months of 1914, and for us at Hinges it was the same routine day after day.

In October 1917 the Austrians, reinforced by picked German divisions, routed the Italians and threatened Venice itself. The British Sixth Army, commanded by General Gough, was despatched from France to assist the Italians and the XI Corps was ordered to get ready to leave for Italy the following morning.

We celebrated our long stay in Hinges in the evening. We did it with champagne which I had never tasted before and the morning after, when we were feeling its effects, we heard the move had been cancelled. Two or three weeks later, when we had dismissed all thoughts of getting away from France, I was sent for by Major Codrington who told me he was going to Italy to arrange accommodation for the XI Corps Headquarters staff and he had chosen me to go with him as his clerk. We were driven to Bethune station the next morning, together with his batman, and we boarded a train with Paris the first stop.

It was a very different experience to the one I had when the 2/7th Worcester Regiment were moved by train from Le

Paris
November 1917

Havre to the trenches in overcrowded cattle wagons labelled '*40 hommes*' or '*8 chevaux*'.

We stayed in Paris overnight, Major Codrington and his batman went off to an hotel and I slept in a warehouse, near the Gare du Nord, which had been converted into a dormitory for British soldiers.

Three things are indelibly imprinted upon my memory. Firstly, surprise at seeing a collection of beautiful English 'Society' girls looking so fresh, bright and cheerful at one o'clock in the morning, serving coffee, tea and snacks to British soldiers in a canteen at the Gare du Nord.

Secondly, the haircut I had next morning at a Paris hairdresser's shop. I said "Oui" to everything he asked me and finished up with the whole works, shampoo, haircut, singe and goodness knows what else. I smelled like the inside of a French parfumerie.

The third surprise was the ride in an open army truck from the Gare du Nord, across Paris, past the magnificent Opera House, to the Gare de Lyon station.

I have been to Paris many times since, but that first trip still remains the most impressionable in my mind.

We entrained for Italy on the night train with a well-stocked basket of food for our sustenance. When dawn broke the next morning, the train was speeding alongside the magnificent French Alps, the first real mountains I had ever seen. The wild and fantastic scenery struck a romantic note in my young mind, especially the black caverns at the foot of the lonely range of mountains and conjured up thoughts of smugglers and their contraband. At Modane, the border town, we changed into a slow-moving Italian train. The clock on the French platform was an hour different to that on the Italian side. An elderly Italian in our compartment chatted to us in English. He had spent many years in London selling hot chestnuts in winter and ice cream in summer and had returned to Italy to spend his retirement. He told us the streets of Turin, our next stop, were laid out in the shape of a fishbone, one main street and the others leading off at right angles to the left and right.

I thought of that remark fifty years later when my wife and I were flying to the Adriatic for a holiday. It was just after midnight and we were celebrating our wedding anniversary with a small drink when I heard the pilot announce that we were then flying over Turin. I looked down on a maze of streetlights but, alas, I could not make out the shape of a fishbone.

At Verona we stayed long enough to discover a Roman amphitheatre and to chat on the platform of the railway station with a young Italian soldier who, by a strange coincidence, had also spent quite a while in London and spoke English fluently. He knew all our popular songs and he, the batman and myself sang them together on the otherwise deserted platform. He was so excited he came on the train with us and we sang with hardly a pause for at least an hour before he left us at the next stop. I have often wondered how and when he got back to Verona as it was late at night and the Italian wartime service was poor.

When our train journey was over the Italian army loaned us a Fiat car and an army driver, and we were driven through the countryside to a small town, the name of which escapes me now.

We opened our office in the back room of a small private house where I worked and slept. I had my meals alone in a small restaurant nearby. Major Codrington and his batman were in an hotel. It did not seem strange that we were the first British soldiers to set foot in the village. I enjoyed having my meals in the restaurant and the jovial owner seemed to look forward to seeing me. He was soon calling me Frederico.

We had a young Italian office as an interpreter. He belonged to the Bersagliera, the Italian Sharpshooter Regiment, but his nervous features belied the reputation of his regiment. Major Codrington told me one morning that he mistrusted him because he could not look him straight in the face. I had not thought much about that particular assessment of character before and it broadened my outlook on human behaviour.

The arrangements for the arrival of the XI Corps were completed and when my colleagues arrived, they were thrilled with their five days train journey. They made light of the lack of comfort in the railway wagons where they had to sit on the floor and dangle their legs out of open sliding doors and sleep with the doors closed at night. It got really stuffy during the night and it was a great relief to open the doors again in the mornings.

In spite of my own exciting experiences with the Major I felt I had missed the chance of a lifetime when they enthused over the wonderful Côte d'Azure, the blue waters of the Mediterranean, Cannes, Nice and Monte Carlo where they saw throngs of joyful people who gave them gifts of fruit and flowers. I had to wait more than forty years before I was able to travel over the same route and enjoy a holiday in the French Riviera, because when we left Italy the troop train took the XI Corps Headquarters staff back to France by the same route as Major Codrington and I had travelled on our journey from Paris.

My main memories of Italy were the extreme kindness of the Italian people and the intensity of the night bombing by the Austrians, which had been almost non-existent in France. The Italian anti-aircraft defences were very effective, and I saw five Austrian planes shot down in one night which was more than I had seen shot down in France in one year. I went for a walk along a country lane at dusk one day and heard a fluttering sound in the air. Then I saw the wing of an Austrian plane gliding gently to the ground the other side of a fence. The descent was so quiet that it occasioned not the slightest concern. How different it would have been in the Second World War if a heavy bomber had dropped near me.

We were with the Sixth Army, under the command of General Sir H.C.O. Plumer. The combined armies of the British, French and Italians were able to contain the Austrian offensive and then take up strong defensive positions. The XI Corps moved forward as far as Camposamperio, a small town within twenty miles of Venice and Treviso. Treviso was still being attacked from the air and we saw evidence of this when we visited it occasionally, when off duty. One of our respected Staff Majors, a member of a titled family, was shot dead in the street one day. I knew him well because he was appointed President of a General Court Martial and as he had no experience of Court procedure, I was asked to sit beside him at the trial and advise him on points of military law and admissibility of the evidence. With due modesty I am inclined to the opinion that this was the only time in the history of the British Army that a Lance Corporal of an Infantry Regiment has sat with the President of a Court Martial, as an advisor.

Venice was out-of-bounds to combat troops, but our Padre, being a non-combatant, was granted a pass to visit, to the envy of almost every other soldier on Corps Headquarters. It was generally understood that the Austrians had agreed to refrain from attacking the historic town provided that no fighting troops were allowed to enter, thereby preserving its treasures for future generations.

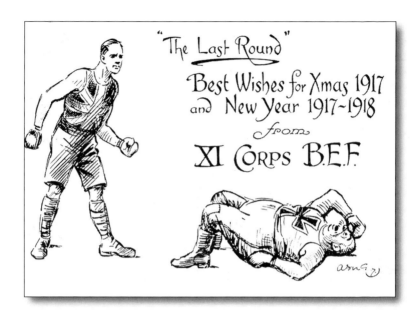

"The Last Round"

Best Wishes for Xmas 1917
and New Year 1917~1918
from
XI Corps B.E.F.

We missed the cooking of Madame at Hinges. At Camposamperio we often had a meal which the local baker prepared for us, and it usually included a delicious dish called 'polenta pudding'. For our Christmas dinner in 1917 we paid him two shillings and sixpence each for a memorable meal which included turkey, polenta and Christmas pudding.

Our two regular army cooks were, to put it mildly, rascals. We suspected our rations were getting smaller and the tastes of those two for the potent local wine were being well satisfied. Confirmation came one morning when there was no breakfast for us. They had got drunk the night before and had flogged our rations to some of the locals. We decided not to report them for the offence, our leniency seemed to do something to them, our rations increased, and we had no further cause for complaint.

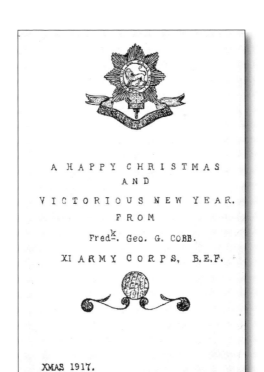

A HAPPY CHRISTMAS
AND
VICTORIOUS NEW YEAR.
FROM
Fred^k. Geo. G. COBB.
XI ARMY CORPS, B.E.F.

XMAS 1917.

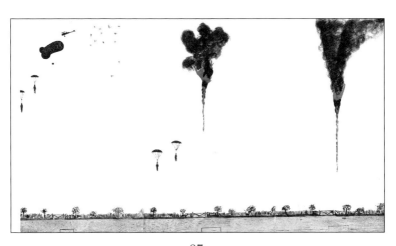

Chapter 7 — World War 1
France, January 1918–January 1919

In the first months of 1918 it was expected the Germans would make tremendous efforts to force a decision on the Western front. They were massing on a grand scale for an offensive against the British and French and had been reinforced by a large number of the Russian army on the Eastern front. To help counter this anticipated attack the XI Corps was ordered back to France after less than three months in Italy.

We travelled by rail in the traditional army style, in box waggons with sliding doors which enabled us to see the countryside and the journey took a week. Image our surprise and pleasure when we arrived back in Hinges and were able to carry on almost as we had left off, including having our meals again at Madame's cottage. This pleasure was not, however, destined to last very long. I could never have guessed when I left our Mess after breakfast one morning that it would be my last walk through the village for more than fifty years.

As I walked back to the château an acquaintance who was in the Intelligence Corps told me that the Germans were going to shell the village at 11 o'clock that morning and when I reached my office packing had already commenced in readiness for the move off.

I have never stopped marvelling at that accurate army intelligence for it was exactly 11 o'clock when the first shell fell in the château grounds and shells continued to explode as we drove away from the cloistered grounds one hour later to a world of great animation.

One or two of our men were slightly wounded by shrapnel but fortunately for us the attack did not reach its full intensity until after we, and the people of Hinges, had departed.

We had seen in the newspapers and journals poignant photographs of refugees fleeing from the terrors of war and now we were witnessing similar pitiful scenes. That sudden enemy attack had forced the humble folk to lock their doors and join long lines of refugees from neighbouring villages who were already tramping in single file along the road to Bethune. Column after column of military vehicles were speeding in the opposite direction on their way to the battle front. The big German offensive had started and the full force of it in our now erupted sector was concentrated on the part of the line held by two Portuguese divisions who broke and fled.

There was one unrehearsed incident on that road which to my mind has never, as a dramatic spectacle, been surpassed at any Royal Tournament performance. A brigade of British Field Artillery was galloping at full speed in the direction of the front line and passed a Portuguese Field Artillery brigade, galloping hell for leather, in the opposite direction in full retreat. The gun carriage and limbers were almost wheel to wheel as they passed each other and I still can see the grim, alert and fixed looks of our gunners on the leading horses as they guided them on a safe, straight course past the Portuguese gun carriages, and more importantly still, past the unfortunate refugees who were almost hemmed in at the sides of the road.

This was the last time I saw Hinges in war time and what a different parting to the one a month or so before when we drove along the dusty and smelly roads of Northern Italy to the railhead where we joined a slow train back to France. The countryside was peaceful and untouched by the War. The womenfolk stopped their work in the fields and waved goodbye in the traditional Italian manner, turning their closed fingers back to themselves as if they were beckoning us to "come back, come back".

How cruel the war had been to France and her people and they had to endure it for another eight months before peace was declared, on November 11th 1918.

Memory has been described as a series of pictures that can be brought out later in life like recordings from the BBC archives.

There were few highlights in those last few months for me. I remember walking alone one afternoon when the stillness of the countryside was broken by an unusual noise in the sky. There was nothing to be seen but the sound passed high overhead and continued on the same plane until distance obliterated it. I never heard that sound again. It was a heavy German shell from 'Big Bertha' on its 60 miles flight to Paris.

As the months passed, I lost the companionship of all those splendid fellows who welcomed me to Hinges in June 1916. The Quarter Master Sergeant was the last to go on promotion to another Headquarters and I was left in charge of the office with a dozen soldiers, many from the last call up, who were willing and co-operative, but inexperienced until a new QMS arrived from Base ten weeks later. In that hectic period there were five divisions in the Corps instead of the usual three and I often worked until the early hours of the morning.

I had two completely different distinctions bestowed on me.

The first was when I was put under 'open' arrest. It happened that a high-ranking officer found some partly burned secret documents outside our Headquarters one morning as he was on his way to breakfast. They should, of course, have been completely destroyed. He sent for the Camp Commandant and they both decided that as I had been on duty all through the previous night, I was the guilty party. The Camp Commandant came into my office and to my surprise placed me under 'open' arrest, ordering me to report to him at 9.00am the next day. I had not had access to the documents and knew it was the responsibility of the young officer on duty who happened to be a member of a distinguished military family and who, I was pretty sure, they would not put under 'open' arrest. I just asked the Camp Commandant to prove the relevant instructions about destroying secret documents had been promulgated to me and, as I anticipated, heard no more about it.

The second distinction was a 'Mention in Despatches' for devotion to duty.

General Foch was appointed Generalissimo of the Allied

Forces and the war in France began to turn in our favour. The Germans were forced to withdraw their battered armies from the territory they had held since 1914 and the last move I made with the XI Corps was to La Madeleine, a suburb of Lille. We were not many miles away and a colleague and I decided to walk. The other members of the DAA & QMG's office went in army lorries and took our belongings with them. We walked across country which was inaccessible except on foot. Whole areas were devastated and scarred with shell holes, trenches and dug-outs were blasted, and concrete defence posts smashed. All that remained of trees were scorched, broken trunks, stripped of branches and leaves; it looked as if the God of War had played all his fiendish cards with one evil earth-ripping throw and all Hell had thundered down.

As I clambered over the unbelievable destruction and devastation I spared thoughts for the unfortunate soldiers who had endured such inhuman suffering and those who had died or had been wounded in that terrible inferno and I offered up a silent prayer to the Almighty for I knew that, but for his wonderous grace, I too might have been one of them.

We walked through the gates of Lille and on to La Madeleine, where smiling women and children waved to us from open doors and windows and told us we were the first British soldiers they had seen since the German occupation in 1914. That suburb of Lille had not suffered any structural damage, the houses looked homely and inviting and it seemed to my companion and myself an opportune time to try and find a comfortable billet. We approached a family who were waving from an open window and they let us have a nice bedroom with a comfortable double bed. We were in clover until my companion caught flu' which had killed many of our troops in France and had spread alarmingly through Great Britain.

Not long afterwards people from town and suburbs went wild with joy, dancing, singing and linking arms in a grand parade up and down the main road from Lille in celebration of the signing of the armistice on November 11th 1918.

Serial No 8196

CERTIFICATE of* Discharge / ~~Transfer to Reserve~~ / Disembodiment / Demobilization on Demobilization.

Army Form Z. 21.

Regtl. No. 202553 Rank. Cpl

Names in full. Cobb Frederick George
(Surname first)

Unit and Regiment or Corps from which *Discharged/DISEMBODIED/Transferred to Reserve. Warwickshire Regt

Enlisted on the. 4th November 1914

For. Warwickshire Regt
(Here state Regiment or Corps to which first appointed)

Also served in. Nil

†Medals and Decorations awarded during present engagement. Nil

*Has/Has not served Overseas on Active Service.

Place of Rejoining in case of emergency. Warwick Medical Category. A1

Specialist Military qualifications. Nil Year of birth 1896

He is *Discharged/Transferred to Army Reserve/Disembodied/Demobilised on 15 March 1919 in consequence of Demobilization.

Signature and Rank.

Officer i/c Records. Warwick (Place)
* Strike out whichever is inapplicable. † The word "Nil" to be inserted when necessary.

N.B.—Any person finding this Certificate is requested to forward it to the Secretary, War Office, London, S.W.1, in an unstamped envelope.

WARNING.—If this Certificate is lost a duplicate cannot be issued. You should therefore take care that it is not lost or mislaid.

---

qualifications as shewn in A. B. 64.

Special Remarks as to qualifications, work done, or skill acquired during service with the Colours. This is required as a help in finding civil employment.

Employed as Clerk at Corps Hdqrs for 2½ years. Capable and Trustworthy.

Soldier's Signature (for identification purposes). Signed (Rank)
Commanding (Unit)

The object of this certificate is to assist the soldier in obtaining employment on his return to civil life. The form will be completed as soon as possible in accordance with Demobilization Regulations.

As soon as signed and completed it will be given to the soldier concerned and will remain his property. He should receive it as early as is compatible with making the necessary references in order that he can either send it home or keep it in his possession.

One form will be issued to each man, and no duplicate can ever be issued.

(7 B) W6938—GD1389 5,000,000 10/18 HWV(P508). Army Form Z. 18.

CERTIFICATE OF EMPLOYMENT DURING THE WAR.
(To be completed for, and handed to, each soldier.)

A soldier is advised to send a copy rather than the original when corresponding with a prospective employer.

It is particularly important that an apprentice whose apprenticeship has been interrupted by Military Service should have recorded on this form any employment in a trade similar to the one on which he has been engaged during such Military Service.

Regtl. No. 202553 Rank LCpl A/Cpl

Surname COBB.

Christian Names in full FREDERICK GEORGE GOODSON

Regt. R Warwickshire Regt Unit attd XI Corps HQ

1. Regimental Employment.

Nature of.	Period.
(a) Training	From 4.11.14 To 23.5.16
(b) In Action (France)	23.5.16 - 16.6.16
(c) Clerk at Corps	16.6.16 Date
	H Qrs.

2. Trade or calling before Enlistment (as shewn in A. B. 64)

Group. 31. Railway Clerk Code 178.

3. Courses of Instruction and Courses in Active Service Army Schools, and certificates, if any.

(a)

(b)

(c)

(d)

The trade or calling must be filled in by the O.C. Unit from the Appendix to Special Army Order No. 6, of 21st October, 1918 (329 of November, 1918).

My Demob Papers

I lost no time finding out how quickly I could get demobilised and soon produced a letter from my employers to show that a job awaited me. I arrived home for good in February 1919, four years and four months after I had joined the army thinking I was in for a short holiday.

We did not get a new suit given to us like the soldiers in the Second World War. I had to buy mine and also numerous other articles of clothing to replace those I had grown out of. Bang went my gratuity of fifteen pounds. The War was costing the British taxpayer one million pounds a day but none of that drifted into the banking accounts (if any) of the British tommies. The munition workers fared better. One of them boasted to a soldier on leave from fighting in France "I could paper the walls of my living room with one pound notes." It did not disturb me when I got to hear about it for if I had not gained worldly riches, I had acquired a wealth of experience and a belief in my own capabilities.

Lord Stokes wrote that the First World War provided him with a crash course in psychology. It provided me with the opportunity I would not otherwise have had, of working with many who had been educated at colleges and schools above the level, but not in my opinion above the standard, of my old Thorpe Hamlet School and I had been modestly surprised and gratified that I could hold my own with them.

It was a fitting climax when the War Office sent me an oak leaf emblem and a certificate signed by Winston S. Churchill, Secretary of State for War, which recorded that I had been mentioned in a Despatch from General Sir H.C.C. Plumer, GCB, GCMG, CVO, ADC dated April 18th 1918. The last paragraph read "I have it in command from the king, to record His Majesty's high appreciation of the services rendered" and it was worth more to me than the gold watch I received from British Railways years afterwards which was inscribed "F.G.G. Cobb, 45 years' service". After such a long period of loyal service I felt that they should have had the graciousness to have worded the inscription "In appreciation of 45 years' service".

T.F./140

The War of 1914-1918.

202555 Pte. (A./L./Col.) E.G.G.Cobb, 2/7th Bn., Worcesters.R. (T.F.)

was mentioned in a Despatch from

General Sir H.C.O' Plumer.G.C.B.G.C.M.G.G.C.V.O.A.D.C.

dated 18th April 1918.

for gallant and distinguished services in the Field.

I have it in command from the King to record His Majesty's

high appreciation of the services rendered.

Winston S. Churchill

War Office
Whitehall S.W.   *Secretary of State for War.*
1st March 1919.

94

Chapter 8 — Civilian Again

It was wonderful to be back in the family fold and the joy of my family was complete when brother Reg came home from Egypt some months later.

I had exchanged letters regularly with my Saxmundham girlfriend which then blossomed into her thoughts of the thrill of an early marriage. I was happy when she found a position as an assistant in a Norwich jeweller's shop and 'digs' near my home but I had no inclination to settle down as I wanted to catch up on the four lost years of my youth by combining courtship with meeting old friends as they drifted back from the war. This arrangement seemed to work satisfactorily until the day I saw a nice new motorcycle in a shop window in Prince of Wales Road and impetuously went inside and bought it. The idea of owning a motorcycle had not entered my head until that moment, and I had not even sat on the saddle of one.

I asked my friend, Arthur Payne, to collect it for me and there is a film stored in my brain that records almost every detail of the scene on Prince of Wales Road that afternoon in 1919 when Arthur and I walked from Thorpe station after we had finished work at 5.30pm. which was, and still is, the peak traffic period of the day. Crowds of sedentary workers passed us on their way to the station to catch their trains to the dormitory towns (the railways had the monopoly then). Cyclists in their hundreds and an occasional motorcyclist were riding home from their daily work at Lawrence and Scott's, and Boulton and Paul's factory.

I watched with pride as Arthur wheeled the shining motorcycle across the busy road and started off in the other line of traffic towards Thorpe station. Suddenly, to my horror, rider and machine shot forward at terrific speed, and

I had a dread feeling of apprehension for their safety as they disappeared from view, past double processions of Great Eastern Railway horse drawn vehicles that were on their way to the station. There were pair horse vans with the drivers perched almost on top of the vans, single horse parcel vans and goods trolleys that had been delivering and collecting railbourne traffic in the city all day long at a leisurely pace and now, finding themselves on Prince of Wales Road, every horse seemed to sense it was the last journey of the day. They threw off their lethargy and, urged on by their drivers, raced each other at breakneck speed, wheel to wheel, towards Thorpe station where their well filled nose bags awaited them. It was like an exciting chariot race and how relieved I was when I turned the corner of my road and saw the motorcycle propped up against the curb of the pavement outside my house, safe and sound, as Arthur had left it. He told me afterwards the accelerator lever on the handlebars worked in the reverse way to that on his own motor bike and when he thought he was slowing down he roared off at full speed. It seems like a fairy story when we read that more than 1,400 motor vehicles passed along Prince of Wales Road in one hour peak traffic peak period in 1970 and goodness knows what the count would be today.

I had bought the motorbike on the spur of the moment without consulting anybody and my fiancée was not impressed either with the machine, or my stories of wonderful rides to the seaside and Norfolk beauty spots. She told me it was obvious the money I had wasted would put off the happy day, and that she was anxious to wear a wedding ring instead of selling them. So, she packed up her trunk and went off to her sister in London and to the second string of her bow.

It was twenty years before I found out what happened after that unemotional parting. I was working in Ipswich as an outdoor representative of the railway when I saw three attractive young ladies walking towards me. One of them was smiling and when almost level with me detached herself from her companions. It was her, as good-looking and neat as when I last saw her. We chatted cordially, exchanging

96

news of our respective families. We were both married with families and living at opposite ends of the town. We did not mention our youthful association but seemed mutually to accept that phase in our lives as steppingstones to the happiness it was obvious we were both enjoying. She re-joined her friends and passed out of my life for ever. I was glad we had met to close the chapter.

Chapter 9 — Back to Work in 1919

I was one of the first to return to the office at Norwich Thorpe station where I was welcomed by those I had left behind on the morning of November 4th 1914 when I impetuously walked out of the office bound for the Drill Hall in Chapel Field Road. They had been exempted from military service as the railways were considered an essential part of the war machine.

We were an extremely happy lot, there was not a union member amongst us, and we worked conscientiously without grumble or strife; for one master, the Great Eastern Railway. Those who stayed behind were, naturally, holding the key positions and the years afterwards it was a case of waiting for dead men's shoes so far as promotion was concerned.

My first week's salary was fifty seven shillings and six pence which took a lot of getting used to after four and a half years on army pay which was twelve shillings and three pence a week when I was demobilised.

A new salary structure for railway clerical staff was introduced in August 1919. This provided for five grades. Class 5, maximum of £200 p.a. at 31 years of age, Class 4, maximum £230, Class 3, maximum £260, Class 2, maximum £300 and Class 1, maximum £350 per annum.

My position was classified Class 5 and I immediately appealed for a higher classification. Two years later I received a letter from Sir Henry Thornton, General Manager of the Great Eastern Railway, informing me my post had been reclassified Class 4 with arrears of pay from August 1st 1919. Sir Henry, who was 42 years of age, had been general superintendent of the Long Island Rail Road in Canada and was brought over to England in 1914 by Lord Claud Hamilton, Chairman of Directors of the GER, to put the railway on its feet and, so as far as I was concerned, he had started the right way. My weekly salary was £4.4s.5d and my back pay amounted to £98.1s.4d. which seemed like a small fortune to a young railway clerk.

I found an enterprising way of augmenting my salary by selling tobacco, and cigarettes to the staff and friends, and the business escalated to regular orders from other offices, some outside Norwich.

When I made a personal application to the Inland Revenue Office for a licence it was refused. I was told I must have a shop and the words "Licensed to sell tobacco" and my name displayed over the entrance. I stubbornly requested an interview with higher authority and was taken upstairs to see the Chief Inspector. With youthful zest I was able to convince him I could suitably display the necessary authorisation on the door of the cupboard under my desk which I regarded as my shop, and he granted me a licence. I sold £1,000 worth a year for a number of years. Players were ten pence halfpenny for 20, Gold Flake, Craven "A", Kensitas and other similar brands were eleven pence for a packet of 20.

I was the youngest 4th Class goods department clerk in the Norwich district and was in charge of a sub-section of the General Section. Ted Midlane, who was in charge of the other subsection, had served with the 1/4th Norfolks in Egypt and was in the second battle at Gaza. He was tall, broad shouldered, powerfully built and no one would ever have thought he was a clerk who sat at a desk all day long. On Monday mornings he would regale us with stories of weekend exploits at his village public house, with his mischievous little cousin who was always up to all sorts of pranks with strangers. He would provoke them into an argument which brought the burly Ted on the scene to protect his protege if he thought there was trouble brewing. One look at him was usually enough to prevent any physical contact. In the office Ted was the acme of politeness and an excellent colleague. His mother was licensee of the Woolpack in Golden Ball Street which was demolished to make way for the more imposing public house bearing the same name. The artist Sir Alfred Munnings visited the Inn when he was an apprentice with Roberts, the printers, and Ted often mentioned that the stableman who held the horses in some of Munning's paintings was a regular customer.

Ted's assistant was the son of a country parson. I wish I could relate to the reader how the young man, not long from school, brought a Catholic respectability to the office in general, and to Ted in particular, but it cannot be done. To our surprise and amusement, we very quickly discovered the range and rapidity of his swearing would almost make a Navvie blush. He was obviously a square peg in a round hole and left the railway service after a while to go on the stage, but he was never forgotten, especially the time when I organised a concert in St. Matthews Parish Hall to raise funds for our football club of which I was a playing member. Billing himself as "The Great Carlino" he performed conjuring tricks, one of which was to extricate himself from a large sack. A member of the audience and myself went onto the stage, tied his hands and feet together with rope; helped him into the sack and then tied up the mouth of the sack. We made a good job of it and were walking off the stage when we heard him shout "You've tied up my hair". We had to untie the sack to release his long hair and tied it up again so that he could eventually emerge in triumph. There was another technical hitch at the concert. I was in the wings when the local comedian, Tom Ellis, was giving his turn and I thought how well he was doing. The women in the packed audience were rocking in their seats with laughter. Then I noticed that Tom had forgotten to do his flies up, the more they laughed the more he was animated with success and the more he revealed until I beckoned him off the stage from the wings to make the necessary adjustment.

My Section chief, Billy Payne, was a capable and charming little man with a Kaiser Bill moustache and brushed up teutonic styled hair. The clerks who had filled our places during the war went back to their stations and we settled down as a happy industrious team for more than a decade and we all agreed in later life they were the happiest years of our railway careers.

Billy would proudly demonstrate his athletic ability by walking around the office on his hands and to every newcomer would relate the story of how he wrestled a sixteen stone policeman in the CEYMS gymnasium and left the worthy officer sitting on the floor speechless with amazement.

We never abused his position and he enjoyed with us the harmless banter and leg pulling which increased in intensity when Dick Kahler and Bertie Withers were demobilised and provided with desks in our General office even though they belonged to another Section and their Chief had an office along the corridor. They were thankful there was no room in his office for them, because he patterned his attitude towards his subordinates on that of our old District Goods Manager.

He started on Dick the first morning he joined his Section, calling him "boy" every time he wanted something done. Dick told him he resented the appellation and reminded him "the boy" had held the rank of Quartermaster Sergeant and was married with two children.

On one occasion, a precocious youngster, not long left the City of Norwich School, innocently walked up to the Chief Clerk when he was drinking his morning coffee in the Refreshment Rooms and started chatting to him. When the lad got back to the office he was sent for and told in no uncertain manner never to approach him again. Happily, there was a change for the better in his disposition when his old District Manager retired in 1931.

The new manager was Mr R.R. Pettit, an easy-going sort of man who had started work as a country station clerk and rose to the rank of Superintendent, and assistant to Major Chauncy, Chief of Police, London and North-Eastern Railway at Liverpool Street station. Mr Pettit breezed into the office one day with an avuncular smile and told us his office door was always open if we wished to see him at any time. Some of his personality rubbed off on the Chief Clerk whose marriage to a charming young wife completed the transformation.

I had proof of this soon afterwards when my wife, Irene, and myself were invited to their house for lunch one Sunday.

We were entertained royally and stayed until late in the evening. It seemed incredible my host should ever have refused to let juniors walk across the station yard with him for fear our old Victorian master might catch sight of him from his office window. Such was the psychological effect he had on all his personal staff.

It was some time before we could get used to the different method of approach by Mr Pettit. It was such a complete contrast to the aloofness of the old "Guvnor" who only came near our office once a year. That was on Christmas Eve when he popped his head just inside the door of the General Office with a "Compliments of the Season, gentlemen" and disappeared like a shot out of a gun. A good example of his lack of touch was the time he pressed his bell button to summon the Chief Clerk to his presence. Bertie Withers went along to tell him the Chief Clerk was out and when that 'worthy' duly presented himself, he was asked "Who is that young man who came in to tell me you were out?" He did not know Bertie was a member of his personal staff even though he had been in the office for more than two years; lost a leg in the war and walked with a pronounced limp.

Bertie had a rather monotonous job preparing passenger statistics which did not bring him into the limelight, but a new world opened up for him in October 1927, when, accompanied by Sir Ian Hamilton, he unveiled the Norwich Civic War Memorial in the presence of the largest crowd ever to assemble in and around the Norwich Market Place. Bertie had served with the British Forces in Gallipoli; as they included the 1/4th Battalion, the Norfolk Regiment. At that time the War Memorial was sited in front of the Norwich Guildhall, and in 1938 it was moved to the Garden of Remembrance, in front of the City Hall. Two photos of Private Withers are displayed in the Norfolk Regiment Museum at Britannia Barracks. One shows him at the unveiling ceremony and the other is of his war medals.

I remember my mother coming home from the ceremony tickled pink at a remark she overheard in the crowd. A girl behind her was feeling faint in the crush and her male companion propped her up against the window of a jeweller's shop and was trying to revive her by waving a newspaper in front of her face. Suddenly a woman's voice was heard protesting at the attention the young man was bestowing on his girl.

"Look at him" she shouted, "you can tell they are not married, or he would be fanning her with his fist."

Another office colleague was Dick Kahler, whose family lived at the bottom of Gas Hill. His father kept the baker's shop there. Next door was an old building which comprised half a dozen slum houses that looked onto Bishopgate and the River Wensum. I was told that the occupants could not go to bed without stepping out of their living room door onto a rough dirt path bordered on to the public footpath, then, opening an adjacent street door and going upstairs to bed. The procedure had, of course, to be reversed when they came down to breakfast the next morning. I felt sorry for the hapless occupants particularly on a cold winter's night with the snow ankle deep, or when soldiers from the Cavalry barracks and the 'Norfolks' from the Britannia Barracks, both nearby, were turned out of the fifteen public houses which were all within a few hundred yards of each other.

I remember my father telling me about the Royal Scots Greys when they came straight to Norwich from fighting the Boers in South Africa. They had not seen civilisation and white women for years and they went wild with excitement and drink on their first night out in Norwich. There was fighting over girls in public houses and they spilled out into the streets. At one time the Mayor prepared himself to read the Riot Act but some sort of order was restored and the drunk and battered passed those tenements on their way back to barracks.

I do not think the insalubrious atmosphere of Bishopgate did Dick Kahler any good. He was not at all robust. There were times when the pungent malty odour of beer being brewed at the brewery in Barrack Street mixed with the pleasant smell of the baking of bread in Dick's father's bakery, not unpleasant perhaps, unless the gasworks on Gas Hill, high above the shop, happened to release an acrid sulphurous and obnoxious smelling gas we call "Blue Billy".

That foul smell could be noticed all over the city and its suburbs. Goodness knows what the full blast was like as it descended on the little baker's shop.

For good measure there was the horrible smell which wafted from the other side of the road from the stinking hides that hung on long lines beside a public footpath on Riverside Road at the premises of Ramsay Bros., Fell-mongers, Hides, Skins and Wool merchants. Pedestrians could smell them long before they could see them, and to add to their discomfort, they had to pass a men's convenience belonging to the pub next door which mercifully has now been demolished together with the premises of Ramsay Bros..The baker's shop, the old tenements and a pub named "The Marquis of Granby" were pulled down to make way for road widening and "Blue Billy" ceased to raise choruses of "phews" from the citizens of Norwich when North Sea oil was introduced.

Barrack Street between the wars

Courtesy Norfolk County Council

As I write, in 1973, Steward & Patterson's Pockthorpe Brewery is being demolished and never more will the good old Norfolk ales and stout be brewed in the neighbourhood. The big brewers have cast their net.

Cavalry Barracks and Steward & Patterson's Pockthorpe Brewery

Courtesy Norfolk County Council

Barrack Street was, by common consent, the roughest locality in Norwich especially on Saturday nights when policeman patrolled through it in pairs. There was a brewery, public houses and the cavalry barracks on one side of the narrow street and on the other side more pubs and a row of mediaeval houses, the front doors opening onto the footpath. They were of the same architecture as many that have been preserved in East Anglia but less attractive and more neglected; the walls begrimed with an accumulation of centuries of dust and dirt and bespattered with mud thrown up by passing vehicles. Flemish weavers were said to have made their cloth in the upstairs rooms which protruded well beyond the walls of the ground floor rooms.

In my courting days I had to walk through Barrack Street late at night on my way home, and fights and rough houses were frequent. I always heaved a sigh of relief and breathed in the fresher air when I had passed the last three pubs from whence came the sounds of revelling and ribaldry which increased in volume when the doors were opened, and an almost overpowering fug of foul air, stale tobacco and beer was emitted.

There was a marked improvement when the 12th Lancers came to the Cavalry Barracks, Norwich, a year or two before the First World War. They were well disciplined and well-behaved and thanks to the popularity of the Band, under the conductorship of Major Starkey, the regiment became part of the life of the City of Norwich so much so that the Major was presented by the City with a portrait of himself in oils, which was hung in St. Andrews Hall. It was a great attraction to citizens to listen to the band playing in the Barrack Square every Sunday morning, either from a "ringside" position or, as I preferred it, from the slope of St James Hill which was an excellent vantage point.

In August 1914 the 12th Lancers went off to join the other Old Contemptibles in France, soon to be without their horses, and the barracks were renamed the Nelson Barracks. Since that time the planners have been at work and the street is now the acme of respectability. The mediaeval houses have been replaced by council flats which stand well back from the wide trunk road that has been built to take vehicular traffic to and from the North and Midlands to Great Yarmouth and Lowestoft. The high wall of the barracks has disappeared and a grassy slope fringes new houses standing on the extensive site of the demolished barracks. For better or for worse only five out of the fifteen public houses are left in the neighbourhood.

Chapter 10 — The Golden Years

My golden years commenced at the age of twenty-three. I enjoyed riding my new motor bike on the open road, and they were really "open " in the year 1919. There were few other vehicles to distract one's attention and the only hazards were the roads themselves, surfaced as they were with sand and tiny flints that caused punctures galore in tyres that were far inferior to present-day standards.

I did not have one of those big, powerful, Indian motorcycles that used to roar past like a red tornado but a modest Excelsior with a 2½ horsepower Villiers engine with no kick starter. You had to push and run to get the engine to start and then jump on the saddle quickly. The first time I tried it, I threw myself off the saddle again, just as it reached the wheel of a horse and cart that was passing along the main road. It was a near thing, and the old man in charge stopped long enough to call me all the choicest names he could think of, laced with swear words, which I well deserved. It taught me to be careful.

In the streets of Norwich there was no real evidence of the changing pattern. The general opinion amongst traders and industrialists was that the horse was the ideal motive power for delivery and collection services and that motor vehicles could not satisfactorily negotiate the narrow streets and the approaches to factories.

The District Goods Manager of the Great Eastern Railway, who controlled the large fleet of horse drawn railway vehicles, held this view very strongly and was sceptical when his head office in London sent two army surplus 30 hundredweight Shefflex motor lorries to Norwich. They were to be tried out in the city for the collection and delivery of rail traffic, to decide if they could profitably replace horse-drawn vehicles. The cost of a horse and vehicle had been worked out at £1 per week and a motor lorry at the equivalent of two and a half horses. The experiment was an economic and operational success and as motor lorries gradually replaced the horse teams there was an awareness that the wind of change had reached East Anglia.

With the advent of the cheap family car, the motor industry began to expand. Thousands of army surplus motor lorries were bought by demobilised soldiers with their gratuities and used for short hauled goods and parcel traffic in towns and villages.

Railway management was complacent about the development of the internal combustion engine. The Railway magazine of 1919 printed an article which said, "Of the various methods of transport now working in conjunction with the railway industry there is no closer ally than that of road motoring". What a false prophet the writer turned out to be when he went on to extol the great advantages road transport would provide for the railways — "There is little doubt" he wrote "but that British railway companies will avail themselves to a greater extent than heretofore of the facilities offered by the road motor passenger car and the road motor goods lorry for the performance and necessary work in feeding the trunk railroad lines of Great Britain with traffic"…" For goods traffic the motor lorry is an excellent jackal for the railway lion".

Then the railways started feeding "excellent jackal". They introduced a country collection and delivery service at stations where they had no cartage vehicles of their own, and appointed small, mostly one man and one lorry, cartage agents to collect traffic for dispatch by rail from senders in the neighbourhood of the station and to deliver railborne traffic. It was like 'manna from heaven' to those small haulage men, many of whom had bought an army surplus motor lorry with their gratuities after the First World War. They were able to find out exactly what traffic was moving in their locality, to skim the cream of railway traffic by selecting what could profitably and efficiently be conveyed through their own vehicles, and then to quote rates lower than the existing rail figures. There are still, I imagine, haulage operators alive today, who regularly admit it was the railway that put them on the road to success.

On the passenger side, the United Automobile Services Ltd. was formed as far back as 1912 to take over the service in East Anglia which had previously been operated by none other than the Great Eastern Railway, including the motor bus service between Norwich Thorpe station, Loddon and Beccles. For some years the headquarters of the United Automobile Services were at Lowestoft but were moved to York in 1926.

They commenced to operate passenger services from Norwich, Great Yarmouth, Lowestoft, Cromer, and Kings Lynn and developed to such an extent that in 1930 they carried 10,000,000 passengers with the fleet of 220 vehicles. It was in the same year we humble clerks were apprehensive for the future well-being of the railway when we saw, from our office window at Norwich Thorpe station, the cabmen's shelter and a large oval shaped shrubbery were being removed from the extensive station forecourt to make way for a large omnibus station with a covered platform to protect bus passengers against the weather. This was for the United Automobile Services who later merged with the Eastern Counties Company to form the Eastern Counties Omnibus Company with headquarters at Norwich.

The railways had adopted a policy of co-operation with omnibus companies throughout the country and a situation of great importance to the railways occurred in 1929 when they obtained parliamentary powers to operate their own road motor vehicles and to enter into agreements with road transport undertakings. This power enabled the London and North Eastern Railway to acquire shares in the Eastern Counties Omnibus Company although their financial interest was not a controlling one.

That cabmen's shelter, victim of progress, had provided us with plenty of fun. From the office window we used to see an old lady trot through the station entrance from Prince of Wales Road about the same time every morning, go around to the side of the shelter where she thought she could not be seen and stand and 'relieve her feelings'. She wore a long black skirt and reminded me of the old women in Hinges, in northern France, who would rush out of church on Sunday morning and do the same thing just outside the door of the church. I got used to that after a while but I, and other young soldiers who were with me, were really surprised and shocked the day we saw a young French soldier, home on leave, walking arm in arm with his girl. Regardless of our presence they both stopped in the middle of the road and without even unlinking arms he proceeded to 'spend a penny'.

Norwich Thorpe station was built in 1885/86, to the design of William Ashbee and John Wilson, and by the famous contractor; Sir Morten Peto. It is an impressive building, now Grade II listed. There was a standard type of desk fitted at Norwich Thorpe and in every Great Eastern Railway office. The desks were built in rows according to the size of the office; on a high framework, with sloping tops so that the clerk could write standing up or sitting on a high stool. As one can imagine they were somewhat antiquated. I sat on a high stool by a window which gave me an unrestricted view of the whole of the station forecourt, I could work and still be conscious of the comings and goings of the outside world. Therefore, I had a grandstand view through the years of the arrivals and departures of members of the Royal family and other high dignitaries who came to Norwich on official visits.

The most memorable one to me was when Edward, Prince of Wales, came to Norwich in 1923 to officially open the new Carrow Bridge. From an office window inside the station I saw him step out of a train onto Platform No.1, shake hands with the Station Master; who was dressed in frock coat and tall hat, and after being introduced to County and City representatives, I watched the procession come down the platform and past my father, who was standing on duty at the barrier. Rushing back to my desk, I looked down from the open window onto the corn coloured head of the Prince of Wales, who stood, bowler hat in his hand, on the pavement below. His entourage was standing a little removed behind him and he looked very much alone as he awaited the arrival of an official car. He was handsomely attractive, and the people of Norwich took him to their hearts that day; many a girl being heard to murmur "Oh! Isn't he lovely!"

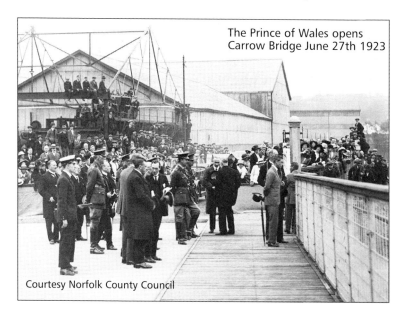

The Prince of Wales opens Carrow Bridge June 27th 1923

Courtesy Norfolk County Council

I literally sat over the gateway of Norwich. Cavalrymen; their horses and guns; exhibits for Cattle and Agricultural Shows, elephants, giraffes, Circus Grand Tops, you name them, they all passed by under my window. The most interesting of all was the fat stock that arrived by train for the Norfolk and Norwich Christmas Association's annual exhibition held in the Agricultural Hall which is now occupied by Anglia Television. The exhibition was the first of three important shows held in Great Britain at Christmas time every year, the others being held in Birmingham and Smithfield. In 1930 at the 51st annual exhibition, one hundred and twenty-six cattle, thirty sheep and forty-six pigs from all parts of the country were exhibited and 7,346 persons passed through the turnstiles. His Majesty King George V, the patron of the show, secured premier honours in its class for a Red Pole Steer. The fat bullocks exhibited weighed twice as much as those now being bred by modern breeders. I recollect one beast, named "Tiny Tim", who was so heavy the floorboards of the cattle float in which he was to be moved from the station to the show collapsed under its weight of twenty five hundredweight. At the end of the Show there was keen competition among Norwich butchers to purchase the exhibits, so to provide prime Christmas fare for their customers. The Christmas displays in the shops of the principal butchers, including W.J. Algar and Mark Stockings, both in St Stephens Street, and William Chaplin in Prince of Wales Road, (names gone but not forgotten by those of my generation), were great attractions for city shoppers. The shop fronts, except of course for the doorway, were completely covered with rows of whole sheep, pigs and huge sides of beef, each bearing a large card showing the honours the beast had gained at the Show and the name of the illustrious owner. Imagine the epicurean thrills that ran through the household when the joint of beef from King George V's winning Red Poll steer was placed on the Christmas dinner table.

How often a word expressed or written invokes the remark 'that reminds me'. It happens to me now that I think of that cabmen's shelter which had outgrown its usefulness when the poor old cabmen were pushed out by the arrival of the motor taxi cabs. Two old 'Jehu's', 'Towser' Woodcock, who hailed from beside the river at Thorpe St. Andrew, and 'Rort' Morris from the Barrack Street area, stuck to their licences for quite a while, their cabs standing for hours on end on the rank inside the station; the cabbies sleeping peacefully inside their cabs and I suspect the horses were sleeping too. It was a real occasion when one or other of them secured a 'fare'. 'Rort' was the last to go.

There were other eyes other than mine watching the passing of the cabbies. They were the pigeons that had built their nests and reared their young on the ledges of the high wall just above the hackney carriage stand inside the station; from which position they could wistfully regard the nosebags of the cab horses. Pigeons had established themselves there, practically since the station was built, and in

1910 some members of a splendid flock of purebred fantails, kept by an ecclesiastic in the cloisters of Norwich Cathedral, forsook the quiet seclusion of the cloisters, the lofty spire, the pinnacles, and the gargoyles, for the noise and bustle of Norwich Thorpe station. The birds that looked down on the deserted cab rank greatly resembled the breed in colour and shape except they had ordinary tails. Happily, they found a benefactor. At 11 o'clock every morning they strutted proudly on the high ledges, strangely alert. There was a mild fluttering of wings as if they were tuning up for flight and then with one accord, they would glide gracefully down to a rather unobtrusive looking elderly man standing on the circulating area. Some pigeons were using his head and shoulders as a landing ground and others trotting expectantly at his feet. He had made a hobby of feeding the birds since he retired from railway service many years before, and by patient endeavour got to know each one by its characteristics. It never failed to amuse both young and old and it seems a pity when they were all driven away from the station premises, never to return.

When I returned to the railway in 1919, I was agreeably surprised at the number of social events that were organised for the entertainment of the staff. They were, in the main, concerts held in the old Ethel Road School Hall, organised by Gordon Bayfield who was chief staff clerk in the District Superintendent's office. He was the pioneer of staff social clubs in Norwich and by his untiring efforts the GER Social Club was formed with headquarters on Thorpe Road. The Ailwyn Hall was built soon afterwards. I look back on years of happy associations with the sporting and social activities. The railway authorities were generous with free rail passes for competitors in sporting events and we found ourselves travelling to different places competing in swimming and football competitions.

I was a member of the very successful football team, which won the Dann Charity Cup in 1921. We also played against Norwich City Reserves on October 21st 1920 in an historic match for which the members of the team were given the afternoon off to play.

Norwich *GERFC — Great Eastern Railway Magazine*

We drew the match 2–2 which surprised our railway supporters and I scored the first goal! It was historic because it was in that game that the popular, long serving, Joe Hannah* made his very first appearance for Norwich City.

As a secretary I often attended meetings of the GER Amateur Athletic Association in London, travelling with a free pass, of course, and after the meetings which finished early in the afternoon, I would wander round London, returning to Norwich by a late train. On one occasion, in October 1923, I found myself outside Olympia and bought a ticket from a tout for fifteen shillings, which seemed a great extravagance in those days when salaries were low. It was for the fight between Joe Beckett, the British Heavyweight champion and the famous Georges Carpentier. Beckett seemed very self-assured and 'cocky' as he waved to the crowd before the start of the fight but 90 seconds after, it was all over. Before I hardly realised it had commenced,

---

*James Henry (Joe) Hannah made his debut for the Norwich City first team on January 13th 1921. He went on to make 427 appearances and famously was so disgruntled with his performance in a match that he 'sentenced' himself to walk home the twenty five miles to Sheringham.

FOOTBALL.

NORWICH CITY RES 2, NORWICH G.E.R. 2.

About 300 persons gathered at the Nest yesterday afternoon to witness the friendly between Norwich City Reserves and the Norwich G.E.R., which ended in a 2-2 draw, a result which reflects credit on the City League side. The spectators showed their appreciation of the plucky display of the Railwaymen by according them most of their cheers. The hero of the match was Wilkinson, a brother of the City half-back, who was in the G.E.R. goal. He gave a good idea of his ability in the first half, and he confirmed good opinions in the second. The crowd showed almost wild delight when Hope, with a penalty kick, shot straight at Wilkinson, and the goalkeeper was able to clear his lines. In the first half the City Res. had most of the play territorially, though the visiting forwards infused a good deal of enterprise into their play, and made the most of their opportunities. It was their determination to let no chance go begging that led to their leaving the field at half-time leading by the only goal. Five minutes before the interval a sharp attack developed on the left, and the ball coming across to Cobb, the latter headed past Staff. The Federation man, who was making his first appearance in the City colours, had no chance. After the resumption the City Res. pressed heavily, and it was a wonder that the G.E.R. goal survived so long. Cheers for Wilkinson's smart work were the chief feature. He got over the penalty kick all right, and the crowd heaved a sigh of relief on his behalf. Irony of fate, it was a mistake of Hammond that eventually resulted in Wilkinson's defeat. Laxton sent a good ball square to the middle, and Hammond, attempting to clear, turned it past his goalkeeper. Later Hannah, the Sheringham centre, who was another new comer to the City's ranks, scored a good goal. Fortune favours the brave, and before the end it came the way of the G.E.R., for Staff could only partially clear after good work on the visiting right, and Stratton put the scores level.

City Res.—H. W. Staff; Hope, Pearce; J. Duncan, W. Duncan, Hopewell; Cowil, Rhodes, H. Hannah, Kidger, Laxton.

G.E.R.—C. Wilkinson; S. Fish, J. Hammond; R. Potter, H. Foulsham, A. Dent; F. Cobb, H. Dewing, A. Mattin, W. Reynolds, J. Stratton.

Yarmouth G.P.O. 9, Y.M.C.A. 1.

Eastern Daily Press – October 22nd 1920

EASTERN FOOTBALL NEWS.

SATURDAY, FEBRUARY 26 1921

Dann Charity Cup
Semi-Finals.

Norwich G.E.R. v. Yarmouth G.E.R.

At the Fountain Ground, Mousehold.
Norwich G.E.R.—G. Wilkinson, C.
Wilkinson, S. Simons, W. Grimmer, H.
Foulsham, A. Payne, F. Cobb, H. Dearing. R.
Potter, A. Mattin, J. Stratton.

Yarmouth G.E.R.—Beckett, Roper, Dunham,
Parker, Smith, Matsill, Tooke, Eagle, Carver,
Neve, Gowen.

The start was delayed to adjust the goal-
posts, and Norwich kicked off facing the wind.
Yarmouth were the first to assume the
aggressive, and Gowen shot past. Norwich returned and Cobb failed when well placed.
Stratton raced away, and after eluding Parker,
put in a perfect centre, but nobody was up to
convert. Tooke showed up prominently in a
smart attack, and essayed a good shot which
Wilkinson dealt with cleverly. A corner
which fell to the Yarmouth men was cleared,
and Mattin led another raid for Dearing to
miss his pass.

Roper displayed his good tackling qualities
and frequently dispossessed the nippy local
forwards. Play was fast and even, each
quintette having a good share of the play.
Cobb placed a corner nicely for Stratton to
head wide. Mattin just failed with a hook
shot a few seconds later. The Yarmouth
keeper had a warm handful in diverting an
express one from Potter, but he completed a
good clearance. Half-time—Yarmouth G.E.R.
0, Norwich G.E.R. 0.

On resuming Yarmouth attacked and Tooke
unaccountably failed when close in for Simons
cleared under the cross-bar. The Norwich
eleven forced matters, and they all but pierced
the Yarmouth citadel. Matsill sent in a
drop shot which Wilkinson cleared. Cobb
raced down and kicked into the centre, and
Parker in his effort to clear kicked the ball
into his own goal. Cobb missed by inches with
a long shot. Beckett distinguished himself in
pushing Mattin's shot round the post. Final—
Norwich G.E.R. 1, Yarmouth G.E.R. 0.

EASTERN DAILY PRESS

SATURDAY, MARCH 26, 1921

DANN CHARITY CUP.

Norwich G.E.R. deservedly won the right to
retain the Dann Charity Cup in the final with
Lowestoft G.E.R. at the Crown Meadow, but
were not so superior as the score of 3 to 1
suggests. Captain Guillaum (Lowestoft Harbour Master) kicked off, and music was supplied
by the Town Military Band. There was little
difference in the merits of the respective teams,
but whereas Lowestoft's forwards were only
prominent in the centre, the display of the
whole of the visiting forwards was good generally. Lowestoft's failure can be partly attri-
buted to the fact that their wing men were
weak, and though they had as much of the
play as their opponents, Winner was the only
one to get through. C. Wilkinson in goal
played a fine game for Norwich. Goals were
obtained by A. Mattin, Dearing, and Potter
from a penalty. At the conclusion of the
game Mr. C. H. Robinson presented the
winning team with the Dann Cup.

DANN CHARITY CUP.
Lowestoft G.E.R. 1, Norwich G.E.R. 3.

Carpentier landed a terrific right to Beckett's jaw which must have been sufficient to finish the fight but as he was falling Carpentier followed up with a quick left and another powerful right to the jaw which laid him out cold.

When I reached Liverpool Street the last train to Norwich had gone long since and I persuaded the Station Inspector to allow me to travel on the newspaper train which left at 3.30am. There were no carriages on the train, and I sat on bundles of newspapers in a goods van arriving home at 7.00am

When I met my usual companion on the way to the office just before 9.00am, the topic of conversation was the sensational fight the night before which provided the headlines in the national newspapers, and he took a lot of convincing that I had actually seen the fight at Olympia.

At one time I took my mother to the British Empire Exhibition at Wembley which was opened by his Majesty King George V and Queen Mary in April 1924. Canada, Australia, New Zealand, India, South Africa, Burma, Malaya and all the rest of the King's dominions and colonies in the far-flung British Empire displayed their arts, crafts, manufactures and products as they were created or produced in their native lands. They each had their separate magnificent pavilions and palaces which had been permanently constructed and were of individual architecture. As an example, South Africa had a diamond washing plant, and live ostriches to give local colour. Great Britain had a palace of Engineering and a palace of Industry. The exhibition covered an area of 225 acres, the cost was said to be about £24,000,000 and it attracted millions of people from this country and from all over the world. There was also a costly amusement park and what thrilled me most, and I confess, really prompted me to make the journey, was the rodeo held in Wembley Stadium which was built specially for the Exhibition and is now well known throughout the world. Mother and I were thrilled to see dare-devil riders trying unsuccessfully to keep their seats on the back of bucking broncos, and other cowboys hanging onto the horns of wildly excited young steers; exerting every muscle in their bodies to halt their mad careering round the arena and eventually succeeding, by sheer strength, to bring the beasts to the ground.

It was a wonderful but exhausting experience and when the day was over and we slumped, tired but contented, into our seats on the return train at Liverpool Street station. Our suits were so thickly covered with dust from some of the fifteen miles of paths at the exhibition grounds that it was impossible to tell they were both navy blue in colour.

There were many other trips to London with my office chums and we had the pleasure of seeing the amazing Arsenal forward, wee Alex James, in his long 'shorts'. He dribbled his way, with the ball at his toe; out of a crowd of opposing football players, who up until then, had obscured him from our view. We ended the day's outing with meals at the Silver Grill at Romano's; the famous restaurant. The cost was well within our modest means and it was all very relaxing after the confines of the office.

It was in 1908 that Colonel William Johnson Galloway, a director of the Great Eastern Railway, founded the GER Musical Society, and by giving his time, energy and personal generosity, he brought it to a high state of efficiency. Concerts were regularly given under his baton as honorary Conductor in the Queen's Hall, and at the Hamilton Hall, in the Great Eastern Hotel at Liverpool Street. In 1920 a branch of the musical society was formed in Norwich and it brought a new interest to about forty railwaymen of different grades in the Norwich district. We were fortunate in persuading Mr W.H. Hunn, Mus. Doc., who resided in Great Yarmouth, to become our choir master and by patient endeavour, skilful training and a certain amount of weeding out of those voices which did not blend; he trained us to such a high degree that we were accepted as active members of the GER Musical Society. We zipped up to London for rehearsals and concerts in the Queens Hall; a Bohemian concert in March, and a Carol concert in December each year before enthusiastic audiences. It was a wonderful experience singing with over 350 voices, supported by 100 in the orchestra. It often stirred my emotions almost to physical tears, especially when the orchestra, inspired by the vigorous conducting of Colonel Galloway and, on one occasion, Sir Adrian Boult, gave dramatic renderings of the 'Hungarian Marches' or 'Peer Gynt'. I shall never forget the effect 'Landerkennung' had on me when all 350 of us sang the closing words, "On to God, On to God," in unison, with tremendous volume, tone and fervency, to the fortissimo accompaniment of the full orchestra. It was electrifying. The concerts were stimulating and no less so with the journey back from Liverpool Street to Norwich by special trains in which we were served with splendid meals and drinks by the hotel department staff through the generosity of Colonel Galloway, and were able to while away the rest of the time playing solo.

When the Great Eastern Railway and other companies were amalgamated to form the London and North Eastern Railway in 1923, the GER Musical Society became the LNER Musical Society, and membership was extended to the other companies. The London choir was augmented by choirs from Ipswich, Cambridge, Norwich, Peterborough, Lincoln, Doncaster, and York. Concerts were given in Leeds Town Hall, honoured by the presence of HRH The Princess Mary and the Earl of Harewood, and attended by the Lord Mayors of Leeds, Bradford, and York. Many other towns were visited, including Newcastle, Doncaster and Norwich, but the most memorable concert of them all was held at the Usher Hall, Edinburgh before a very distinguished and packed audience. It was a colossal task organising the train arrangements, the feeding and the sleeping of nearly 500 persons in the orchestra and choir, who were away from their homes for three days. A special train composed of dining car stock started from Liverpool Street on the Friday, and the other choirs from Ipswich, Cambridge, Norwich, Peterborough and beyond joined en route. All meals were served on the train and the rehearsal and concert were held on Saturday. After the concert we slept in sleeping coaches stabled in a siding in Edinburgh, and on the Sunday morning, after steaming up to the Forth Bridge for a close-up view of the immense structure, we headed for home.

It was a sad blow for the society when Colonel Galloway passed away in 1931. Mr William Whitelaw, Chairman of the LNER and President of the Society became the benefactor, and the last concert I remember at St Andrews Hall, Norwich was presided over by him; with Lord and Lady Ailwyn, and the Lord Mayor of Norwich in attendance. Mr Maddern Williams, the popular conductor of the Norwich Municipal Orchestra, our then choirmaster, shared the work of conducting with Mr Edgar Wilby. I was secretary of the Norwich choir for a number of years, and my last job before relinquishing the position was to arrange a concert in the Assembly Rooms at the Agricultural Hall, now the headquarters of Anglia TV. The choir and local singers were the performers, and such was the keenness of the Norwich public for good music that the whole of the seating capacity of 750 seats was sold.

Chapter 11
Bachelor Fred and The Broads

Four enjoyable years had passed since the day I became (to quote the words of my office chums) "the only man to ride away from matrimony on a motorbike". My friends were married or courting, all except my old friend George who took no interest whatsoever in girls. I liked them all a little, but it was not without personal motive on my part that I persuaded the Programme Committee to agree to the engagement of a young professional soprano to sing at the concert in the Assembly Rooms. We became engaged to be married and for two years planned our future. I bought a plot of land in Lime Tree Avenue (off Harvey Lane, on the edge of Thorpe Hamlet) and the house was in the process being built when she was invited to sing at a musical festival in a Norfolk town. I accompanied her on most of her engagements at concerts in the city but on this occasion, she went alone as she had to be away from Norwich for a whole week. It turned out to be the old, old story of the handsome and talented leading young man sharing with the leading lady, who happened to be my fiancée, the exacting rehearsal, the thrills of success at the choral performances and the pleasure of each other's company for the remainder of the week. I can never understand what made me visit my tailor on the Saturday afternoon following her return home instead of going to see Norwich City play. I had not missed a first team match for years and my friends were amazed when I told them I would not be going with them. When I left the tailor, I decided to call at my fiancée's home and show her some patterns. Her mother told me she was out with the leading man and the next morning I walked away from her house the last time with a sad heart and the engagement ring in my pocket.

I was disillusioned to say the least and resolved to remain a bachelor the rest of my life. I had a delightful holiday in Switzerland. What a difference there was between the holiday atmosphere in 1926 and the present time when thousands and thousands flock across the English Channel every week on package tours. The majority of visitors in Lucerne were Germans, who were extremely courteous and correct in manners and dress. Everybody dressed for dinner in the hotels and none could gain admission to the casinos if they were not in evening dress. It was a wonderful start to a new mode of living which I soon found had great advantages.

I was glad of the companionship of my faithful friend George and the comfort of my home where my devoted mother and sisters waited on me "hand and foot". Brother Reg had married long since so I had no competition for their attention. I had been told by an old French country woman in an isolated establishment somewhere on the Western front, truth about myself years before. I was drinking a cup of coffee one morning and the old woman, who was bent in stature and her face wrinkled like a walnut, was telling me how hard she had to work when she was young and how her daughter, who was pregnant and awaiting the doctor, was being pampered. In her time, she said, women had their babies and went to work in the fields later the same day. Her worn appearance seemed proof that she was not exaggerating. I told her about my own life at home and she told me in her patois tongue that I was an *"enfant gâté"* which I found out meant "spoilt". I realised, after giving her words a little thought, that she was right.

There was no need for me to continue saving for the happy day and I was able, instead, to indulge my liking for good clothes. I rigged myself out with a suit for every day of the week and bought the first pair of Oxford Bags from Herbert Duncan, the little tailor of sartorial elegance, whose shop was at the corner of Cow Hill in St. Giles Street. I wore them for the first time on a windy day and the legs were so wide they flapped about like huge pillow slips and were so

Bachelor Fred

conspicuous I took them back and had several inches taken out of each leg.

George and I went to the Spring Gardens in Mountergate Street every Saturday evening in the summer months where we were entertained by concert parties brought to Norwich by Horace Rose. I never forgot his name after hearing a comic come out with the quip "Horace Rose sat on a pin. Horace rose". There was a different concert party each week and at one show Claude Hulbert made his very first appearance straight from University. He wore a brown tweed plus four suit like the one I had. He was so unpredictably funny he had the cast 'in stitches' as well as the audience. It seemed obvious he would make a name for himself with such natural talent.

At the interval every one of the large audience took delight in walking round the huge mulberry tree, the spacious lawn and the paths leading down to the river. We would acknowledge pleasant greetings from acquaintances as we passed and re-passed each other in the enchanting gardens, and they included my ex-fiancée and a girlfriend who were there every Saturday evening, which seemed to indicate her romance was rather short lived.

Dancing at Snellings in Rampant Horse Street where Woolworths now stands was a great attraction. Dancers had to walk through a pastry shop to reach the dance hall. It was a compact, little room with full length mirrored walls and a floor space so small one of my party cracked a mirror with the back of her heel as she was being swung round in the Lancers. A larger hall was built later which boasted to have the best floor in the city, an upstairs sitting-out room where it was easy to stand on a chair and take out the electric light bulb to make sitting out more romantic, and a buffet where we entertained our ladies with sherry and chocolate eclairs. It was select and there was always a surfeit of girls to ensure a pleasurable evening, but I always kept my bachelor resolve and went straight home after the last waltz.

I was walking home after a dance early one morning with George Scott, a young policeman, when we passed a police sergeant named Rolf. He was trying the door of Jackson's, the hatters, in London Street, whose catchy advertising slogan "Jackson's boots and hats are fine, 10/6d and 3/9d" was known to every Norwich citizen. George called out a cheery "Goodnight Sergeant" to which the Sergeant replied with some jocular comment about us being out so late. It was a happy repartee which rather took me by surprise coming from a Sergeant who had earned himself a reputation for the record number of arrests he had made of persons disturbing the peace in our city streets.

George Scott soon passed out of my sphere of activity like most acquaintances do when they marry and move from the district where they spent their youth. He was a young constable who had a meteoric rise to the position of Superintendent in the Norwich Police Force, and soon afterwards he left his native City to become the youngest chief constable in the country; later to be honoured with a knighthood. I remember him best as the one who introduced me to the pleasurable sport of sailing. On the way home from the dance he invited me to spend the following Sunday on the Norfolk Broads with him and two friends who were co-owners of a sailing boat. My knowledge of the river had been confined to trips on the 'Jenny Lind,' and the 'Doris,' two pleasure steamers that plied from Foundry Bridge to Bramerton and Coldham Hall, and also to hiring a rowing boat from places like the Dolphin Inn to row with my friends up the crowded River Wensum as far as Hellesdon Mill. The day I spent with those three healthy young men in their sailing boat was an experience entirely different from all the others. It was one of those glorious days we sometimes have in early spring and, as the holiday season was a long way off, we had the River Bure practically to ourselves. As we sailed from our mooring in Wroxham, past thatched bungalows with well-kept gardens, and by woods and meadows, I was enthralled by the unexpected beauty of the scenery, which was as attractive as any in the country. The river was calm and sheltered for the first few miles and the boat glided smoothly and as effortlessly as a swan. I had a feeling of complete detachment from the outside world.

The real thrills came when we turned right, sorry "to starboard", through a gap in the trees and sailed on to a vast expanse of open water which I learnt was Wroxham Broad. It was then the boat seemed to become alive in the strong wind that prevailed, and the crew took up their action stations. The helmsman at the tiller, watching with keen purpose the pennant fluttering vigorously at the top of the mast, became the master of the situation and steered the boat, with the wind in its sails, at great speed across the Broad. It was exhilarating and unforgettable, and our return to the quieter stretches on the river for more sailing and refreshments at the Horning Ferry Inn was no less enjoyable.

I could not stop talking about my trip when I got to the office on Monday morning and even the usual inquest on Norwich City's football match the previous Saturday afternoon had to take second place. There was one fellow who listened with a more practised ear than the rest. He was our office porter, Billy Smith, a likeable and willing man and jack of all trades who happened to spend most of his spare time 'mucking about' with a friend's boat at Wroxham. He said to me "There is a boat for sale at Wroxham which would suit you". Up to that moment the thought of owning a boat had never entered my head but my enthusiasm was at its highest and I asked him if he would go to Wroxham that same evening and find out all about it. His report was favourable and the next evening we both went along to look her over, and I bought her. Billy gave her a new coat of gleaming white enamel whilst still in the boathouse at the Kings Head. He arranged mooring at Loyne's dyke at two shillings and six pence per week and a fortnight later she was in the water, and I had my first lesson in sailing. He had secured for me the services of an old yachtsman who was acknowledged to be 'the father of the Broads' and an expert helmsman. He must have been well known and respected because he showed me an invitation he had received from the Squire and his titled lady to the wedding of their son and to the reception at the Savoy Hotel in London.

He taught me what to do when the wind changed and in a "jibe" which is when the sail swings suddenly and violently from one side of the boat to the other and would knock you overboard if you did not duck in time. When we were almost becalmed he would point to a ripple on the water some distance ahead and tell me we would soon catch the wind. Most exciting of all to me was when I sat with the tiller in one hand, the main sheet in the other, and sailed close-hauled, keeping the speeding boat on a straight course as she heeled and 'showed her bottom'.

I had two lessons from my tutor who told me several times a person never stops learning about sailing. He was, undoubtedly, correct but it made me feel rather frustrated and I determined to have a go on my own. The opportunity came the next Friday, which was Good Friday and a holiday for me from the office. I motorcycled over to Wroxham and managed to get the sail up correctly. After a while I ventured onto the river and sailed about all day feeling confident enough afterwards to ask my family and friends to share the pleasure of the Broads with me.

I had never before realised the wind always drops about the same time every evening, and what a difference it made to a day of leisure when I had to row the heavy craft back to Wroxham!

I soon remedied this when I saw an Evinrude 2½ horse-power outboard motor advertised for sale for £5 under a box number in a journal. I received an answer to my request for further information from an address in Portman Square, London and went up to London by train to have a look at it. I knocked at the front door of an imposing Regency house and it was answered by a rather superior butler who kept me waiting on the step while he went to fetch something bulky in a sack and, with an air of complete indifference and finality, he directed my attention to the sack, and said "It is five pounds". I stood there, conscious that Colonel Galloway, wealthy director of the LNER and generous donor to our Musical Society, had a residence in Portman Square and that I was in the midst of opulence and respectability. I had a feeling the butler would shut the door on me if I had the effrontery to even peep inside the sack, so I handed over the five pounds, carried the heavy load to a taxi, and headed for Liverpool Street station and home. The Evinrude was in good order and when the wind had dropped it was much more fun sitting back in comfort while the boat chugged its way back to Wroxham.

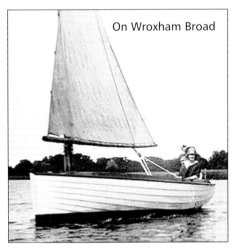
On Wroxham Broad

On the River Bure

George Scott had certainly done me a good turn when he introduced me to sailing, which I found well within my slender means, as the total cost of the boat, together with the launching, painting, primus stove and other equipment, including a new awning and fittings, was under forty pounds. This transformed the boat into a holiday craft in which several could sleep. It was not exactly a "Morning

Cloud" but it served me well. Many photographs of my happy guests on the boat, and on the banks of the Bure, taken with a fifteen shilling No 2A. Brownie box camera, provide me with visual proof that sailing is one of the most enjoyable of all sporting activities whether you possess a boat like that belonging to Ted Heath or a humble half decker like mine.

The Author with sisters May and Rose and Mother
picture taken by brother Reg.

Chapter 12 — Family Matters

I kept my enthusiasm but not my boat, for the time surely arrived when Irene, a sweet young thing of seventeen years of age, smiled at me and my bachelor resolve never to walk out with another girl went "for a Burton". Her lovely face still smiles at me from those photographs and reminds me how ideal the boat was for courting.

I was for ever grateful to the Almighty and to my destiny for steering me through two engagements to be married to a life of sweet contentment, love and understanding that has stood the test of a long married life.

The Happy Day

We three in harmony at 'Lucerne', Lime Tree Avenue

We married on Empire Day in 1928 and went to live in the Lime Tree Avenue house I had built several years previously and had the good sense to let to an office colleague and his young wife who soon found another place to live when they knew I was getting married.

Those early days of marriage seem like a fairy story. We were ideally suited to each other, which the difference in our ages seemed to accentuate, our hair was the same blonde colour and we had the same interests. These were to build our lives around our home, to create a nice garden from a virgin field; and to enjoy the company of our many friends. It was secretly gratifying to me that my parents, and sisters, gave Irene the same genuinely affectionate welcome they gave me, that her youthful charm, radiance and vivacity, enriched their lives. I was equally well-received by her parents, brothers and sisters.

The grocer called a few days after we moved into our new home, to solicit orders, and when Irene, my bride of two or three weeks, opened the door he asked her if her mother was in. He looked embarrassed when she told him she was a lady

131

of the house. He could well have been excused as she looked so young "All peaches and cream" was how a colleague described her to me after he had met her for the first time.

I well remember a year or two later when several of the railway staff, including me of course, were having morning coffee and a chat in the refreshment rooms; one of the group was bemoaning the fact that he was in the doghouse at home and as if to minimise the rift in his family life, he added that every married couple had tiffs now and again. Innocently and truthfully, I interjected that I had never had the slightest difference with my wife, and he turned on me with derision, telling me he did not believe it. I could understand his incredulity because I had many tiffs with the girls I had been engaged to previously so perhaps it was a good thing we did not get married, but Irene was as placid and under-standing as my mother and we found nothing to quarrel about. She saved my life soon after we were married. I could not sit still for very long after I had had my tea and busied myself on jobs outside the house by the light from a 100-watt lamp on the end of a long length of flex connected to the light socket in our bathroom, which adjoined the kitchen. One dark and foggy night, I gripped the flex at a spot where the insulation had perished; the light went out, and 230 volts of alternating electrical current pulsated through the whole of my system. I became absolutely transfixed; unable to move a limb or let go of the flex. I was in complete darkness at the back of the house, a field behind me, and no one to hear me if I shouted for help. I thought it was the end for me and I could not possibly hold out against those powerful series of electric shock from which there was no apparent escape. I knew then why it was called 'alternating current'. I recalled that within the last fortnight, I had read of a woman being electrocuted when an electric fire fell into her bath; and how a man could not release his hold of a garden gate which had become charged with electricity from a faulty cable which hung over a wire fence that joined onto the gate. The unfor-tunate man was electrocuted and the person who tried to pull him off was also killed. I realised I was in the same situation and could do nothing about it.

The good Lord alone knows what made Irene leave her chair in the living room, which was out of earshot, and come into the kitchen. My voice sounded hollow and unreal as I called her to switch off in the bathroom. The pulsating stopped as if by magic. I staggered round the house to the kitchen, my white face pitted with spots and my finger burnt deeply where I had held the flex. My destiny had left it dangerously late.

Soon after this we were awakened about dawn by an unusual disturbance outside the house. It sounded as if scores of wild horses were galloping madly by, then the bed began to shake and the ewer, basin and soap dish on the washstand rattled loudly. It was an earthquake, or an earth tremor would be a better term.

We were young and quick quickly forgot those two incidents. It was about this time Irene's young brother became an assistant car salesman and almost the first thing he did was to try and induce us to buy a second-hand car, which he said would just suit us. It was driven up to our house one Monday evening while we were having tea. It was an old Clyno and looked very smart. The only time I had been in a car was about fifteen years previously, when I was a passenger in a car belonging to the Italian army. The salesman drove me into the country for about twenty minutes, then we changed places and I drove the car with him occasionally holding the wheel from the passenger seat. Funny how one remembers little details after fifty years. The first thing I did wrong was to turn the steering wheel to the left when I wanted to steer the car to the right hand side of the road, which is the direction I would have moved the tiller of my boat. Fortunately, we were moving slowly and there was no traffic about. When we got back to the house, the salesman was in a hurry to keep an appointment, or so he said. I made a diagram of the gear changes, wrote down how to start the engine, how to double-declutch, wrote his cheque for £16.10.00 and the car was mine.

I was impatient to try it out and got up at 5.30 the next morning, followed the written instructions, and was excited when I heard the engine ticking over for the first time. I drove out of my narrow gateway and into the country. The neighbourhood had not yet been developed; houses and cars were few and far between and I had country roads to myself. When I had driven six or seven miles, I decided to do some reversing down a quiet lane and to my dismay the engine stopped and refused to start again. I had heard of motorists running out of petrol; the gauge was not working, but I found there was a small quantity of petrol in a can fixed to the running board. I poured it into the tank and to my joy the engine started up and I got back home safe and sound where Irene anxiously awaited my return.

During the rest of the week I practiced driving up and down the lawn and changing gear when the car was stationary. On Whit Monday in May 1933 I took Irene, my mother and sisters for a long ride. What blind confidence they must have had in me. When we were nearly home, we had to pass Mousehold Aerodrome where all Norwich seem to have congregated to see a 'Great Aerial Display' organised by the Norfolk and Norwich Aero Club. The road in front of me was crowded to a great depth. I drove slowly through as people made a way for me. I could see nothing but human beings all around the car, and when I finally emerged, I felt I had done well for a beginner and my passengers thought so too. They thoroughly enjoyed their very first trip in a car.

The Clyno was a Sedan model, Irene and I sat inside, and my passengers sat on a bench seat in the open boot, facing to the front, their backs leaning against the padded inside of the lid of the boot. The sky was their roof unless it was raining, and then they would put up their umbrellas. They were happy and comfortable, but I admit it would cause much sniggering if seen in the streets of Norwich today.

There were times when some mechanical knowledge would have been useful, like the Sunday morning we were stranded a few miles from Wroxham, unable to start the engine. A passer-by volunteered to ask the nearest garage to send a mechanic. He must have explained our dilemma because, to my amazement, the mechanic arrived with a crowbar in his hand, lifted the bonnet, gave the self-starter a mighty whack and the engine started up first time. I was only charged half a crown for the service, which makes one sigh for the good old days when nowadays we get our repair bills from the garage.

The old Clyno opened up fresh avenues of enjoyment which were not disturbed by the whim of the self-starter to jam very frequently. I took the precaution of carrying a hammer in the car to do just what the mechanic had done.

There came a time when we were cruising peaceably along a country road at about thirty miles an hour and for no apparent reason and without warning, the car started to shake and shudder violently like a bucking bronco. I could feel its crazy and alarming vibrations on the steering wheel and instinctively I knew the only thing that would stop them was to bring the car very slowly to a halt. I learned after-wards it was a bad attack of wheel wobble and the consequences could have been serious if we had been moving at high speed. It never really got over the defect, in spite of the gradual dissipation of my little cache of war savings certificates that went to pay for repairs, and I decided it would have to go, vowing never to buy another second-hand car as long as I lived.

I regretted not being able to take my father on some trips round the countryside he loved so much, particularly to Worstead and Sloley; where he was brought up. He died at the age of 70 years in October 1931; before I had bought the Clyno, and we were proud to read the following tribute to his memory in the *Eastern Evening News:-*

Brother Reg only risked his life on the one occasion I took him from our mother's house in Beatrice Road to my house in Lime Tree Avenue and back again, about a mile each way. When we arrived back, he dashed out the car before it had hardly stopped and slumped himself down on the first chair he could find, exclaiming "Thank God, I'm home". It is a good thing he survived that first car ride with his young brother as he had a very interesting career ahead of him. He left the Norwich & London insurance office in St Giles Street, Norwich when he was appointed junior clerk to the Norfolk

Thorpe Station Figure

THE news of the death, a few days ago, of Mr. John G. Cobb, who for nearly half a century was connected with the old G.E.R. and the present L.N.E. Railway, will be read with regret by thousands of users of Thorpe Station, to whom he was such a familiar figure.

For forty years or more out of his long service with the railway company he was a ticket collector, and in that capacity he was as genial and as popular an official as ever donned uniform.

For the regular traveller he invariably had a cheery greeting, and for the occasional excursionist—more especially in the case of a woman passenger with a young family—an optimistic remark concerning the weather prospects.

Eastern Evening News – November 3rd 1931

Courtesy of the Archant Library

Insurance Committee, formed when Lloyd George introduced the National Health Service in 1914. He married Elsie Brown, the girl next door in Beatrice Road; brought up three children and became clerk to the Norfolk Executive Council with the inception of the Health Service in 1948. He was also Secretary of Princes Street Congregational Church for 25 years until his death in 1964.

Chapter 13 — LNER and Mr Pettit

When Mr Pettit was appointed the LNER's Divisional Commercial Superintendent, Norwich district, in 1930 there had been no promotions in the office since the end of the war and stagnation was likely to continue for many years to follow as the senior clerks were still comparatively young. It had been the same drill for me, year after year, tracing missing goods and parcel traffic, dealing with all coal and cartage matters, preparing statistics and attending to the large daily influx of correspondence which could never be kept up-to-date. We clerks in the General Office all agreed that if we did not have a 'safety valve' we would have been 'bored to tears' with the tedium of routine. Ted Midlane's safety valve was his village pub. Dick Kahler was secretary of the National Deposit Friendly Society. Arthur Knights was district representative of the Provident Mutual Insurance Society and made a good thing out of it. Bertie Withers was a fishing enthusiast. I had my tobacco sales, my home and garden, badminton and tennis. I envied Herbert Lawrence, our outdoor clerk, who never stayed in the office more than a few minutes a day and then was off by train somewhere on the district or careering about on the ex-army dispatch riders twin engine Douglas motorcycle which was sent down from London for his use. For these duties he received Class I salary of £350 per annum, plus £1 per week expenses.

There seemed not the slightest possibility of my being appointed to such eminence, or anybody else in the office, especially when Herbert was promoted to Goods Agent, Great Yarmouth and Headquarters. Liverpool Street sent the LNER District Agent, Liverpool to fill the vacancy, he having just been made redundant.

I even thought Jolly, the rat catcher was a lucky chap. He came into our office every morning for orders, dressed in the uniform of a gamekeeper, his little 'ratting' dog on a leash, ferrets in a wooden box that hung by straps over his shoulder, and a spoon on the end of a stick, which he used to put poison down rat holes. He was Master of his 'profession' which was redesignated "Vermin Destroyer" about the time the title 'Undertaker' and lots of others were uplifted. He travelled by train every day to some station or other, full of confidence and free from supervision or criticism. He was often given permission to work on Sundays clearing rabbits from railway banks and of doing what he liked with those he caught. A few arrived in the office for the senior clerk, until orders came from headquarters at Liverpool Street station that the rabbits should be sent to their office. Jolly duly sent them along but not for long as instructions came that they did not require any further supplies to be sent. We could only surmise that some strange complaint had been rife among "railway" rabbits which had rendered them unpalatable to the London Headquarters staff, and Jolly never let on. His hobby was whippet racing which had been a popular working-class sport for generations past.

I envied the throngs I could see from my office window, walking to and from the station, enjoying freedom and fresh air whilst I was shackled to an office stool. Strange as it may seem, it was a photograph of Norwich Cathedral taken by a professional photographer that was instrumental in giving me my first taste of freedom. The photograph was sent to Mr R. Bell, the Assistant General Manager of the LNER at Liverpool Street station, who in turn, requested Mr Pettit to arrange for one of his personal staff to write an article of not more than 1,000 words on "The City of Norwich" for publication, together with the photograph in the *LNER magazine*. I was asked to do it and joyfully sallied forth into the city, free to roam and return when I had obtained the material I needed.

I did not find it easy and burned much midnight oil before I satisfied myself it was ready for publication but it was well worth the effort for the pleasure in reading my first contribution to the magazine which appeared in July 1929, although credit for the article was given to the Thorpe Station Master, H.C.R. Calver. Mr Bell appeared to be pleased with the article and sent further requests for "write-ups". I had found a fresh interest and a hobby which brought my name to the attention of a great number of railwaymen throughout the LNER system as I was given credit in print for subsequent articles. Mr Pettit encouraged me by inviting me to go with him to Grimes Graves (the prehistoric flint mines) at Weeting, Norfolk, which was my mother's birth-place.

The Ministry of Works had given us permission to visit and we set off one morning in his car. It was an unusual occasion for a junior clerk and caused a mild sensation among my colleagues. I had accompanied the previous District Goods Manager by train when I was his shorthand clerk but had to walk respectfully behind him along the plat-form, his briefcase under my arm and, when in the first-class compartment, to sit silent as a mouse, with my shorthand book and pencil ready for immediate action. He would dictate letters to me at the same speed as if we were in his office, making no allowance for the jolting of the train. I well remember the occasion we were being shaken from side to side in the guard's brake of a fast goods train when it was impossible to write decipherable shorthand curves and strokes, fortunately he signed the letters I subsequently put before him in the office. If I had asked him to repeat a word or sentence there was always the fear in my mind, I would have been banished to spend the rest of my days in a station office. Some who followed me had that sort of experience," You talk too much," he rasped out to one young clerk and packed him off to a station. His successor fared no better when he had the temerity to say more than his situation permitted him to do. The Chief Clerk was immediately ordered to "Get him out of my office at once". It was the best thing that could have happened to him as he left the railway service soon after he had been packed off to the country station and obtained an important situation with the civil service.

My day out to Grimes Graves with the new District Manager was an altogether different experience. The cheery, avuncular, Mr Pettit at the wheel of his car was as friendly to me as Major Codrington had been when we journeyed together in an Italian Army car through northern Italy in the First World War. Both had bridged the gulf between higher authority and the rank and file.

In due time there appeared in the *LNER magazine* an article which I called "Brandon, Suffolk and the oldest industry in the world" which was illustrated by photographs taken for me by Kitty Blandon, whose father was Chief Clerk in the District Superintendent's office.

There was a photograph of the picturesque old bridge over the River Ouse at Brandon with its 'zig-zag' wall approach and its recesses on either side, one rectangular and the other angular, which tradition has it, was so built to prevent mounted pikemen of the middle ages from taking it at the charge. There was also a photograph of the Norwich Guildhall with its fine wall of flints, and another of the exact replica of a flint-knappers workshop which had been installed in the beautiful crypt of the Bridewell Museum in Norwich. We found Grimes Graves in a belt of trees in an isolated part of Weeting. The whole surface of the wood was broken by about 250 circular pits completely overgrown with grass and bracken, with the exception of three pits which the Rev. Canon Greenwell, F.S.A. Durham excavated in 1870. He found them to be ancient flint mines 37 feet deep, 28 feet in diameter at the top and 12 feet at the bottom, where galleries were found radiating in all directions. These appeared to connect a perfect labyrinth of underground passages with other pits in the vicinity. They found Neolithic flint implements, miners' picks made from the antlers of red deer, many of which are now in the British Museum; one still retaining the impression of a prehistoric miner's thumb in the chalky clay which adheres to the surface, also 79 deer's antlers and bones of extinct animals were found. The research not only established a definite link between the flint knapper of 1931,when my visit was made, and the flint worker of the Early Stone Age, but revealed the fact that up to the beginning of the last century the knappers fashioned with a type of stone hammer similar to those discovered in the ancient pits and the modern day flint miner who supplies the knapper with his stones, is digging his pits, and bringing the stones to the surface in the same manner as the prehistoric miner. He is even using the same class of rough chalk receptacle to light the bottom of the shaft, with the exception that the candle replaces the animal fat and moss used in former days.

It was interesting to learn that when the discovery of copper and tin brought the Early Stone or Neolithic Age to a conclusion, the use of the inexhaustible supply of Brandon flints, which was world famous for its spark producing qualities, and its dark rich colour, was continued right through the Dark Ages for obtaining a spark and so making fire and light. The introduction of Flintlock pistols from the continent at the beginning of the seventeenth century added a fillip to the trade; and the tinderbox was also in general use until 1827, when the phosphorus or friction match was invented. Thus, was established a continuous demand for Brandon flints and the craftsmanship of Brandon flint-knappers throughout all this time.

Their services were in constant demand to shape flints for the churches and other buildings for which Norfolk and Norwich are famous. We have excellent examples today in the Norwich Guildhall and the Bridewell Museum, formerly the home of William Appleyard, the first mayor of Norwich in 1403. The north wall of the Bridewell is 79 feet in length and 27 feet in height and is one of the most magnificent specimens of flint-work in East Anglia.

The late Mr W.J. Clarke, in his interesting book on Brandon, gives a comprehensive history of this ancient industry. He tells us that at one time Brandon was the sole source of supply of gun-flints to the British government and two hundred knappers were employed making them for all of the world. In 1931 the demand for flints for the flintlock guns and tinder boxes still being used by natives in West Africa and the Far East provided employment for six knappers. The flints, which were of various commercial sizes, were packed in stout kegs, each containing about 5,000 flints, and dispatched by rail from Brandon station to Liverpool for shipment at the rate of 10 tons per annum.

The industry has died in the march of progress and the Norwich Publicity Association has immortalised it by installing an exact replica of a flint-knapper's workshop in the Bridewell Museum. It is a most interesting and complete exhibit and includes chalk covered stones as received direct from the miner, a bench, hammers, hundreds of finished gun and tinder flints and specimens of different classes of flints for making walls, some diamond-shaped, some square and some round. In fact, it presents to the imagination a feeling that the knapper will shortly return to his stool and carry on with his job, placing the finished flints in the tins on the bench.

I felt honoured when I received a bound copy of the *London and North Eastern Railway Magazine* for the year 1931 endorsed on the inside of the cover "With the compliments of the Chief General Manager". The gift added nothing to the dim prospects of promotion, but it was a pleasing compensation for the many hours I spent preparing the dozen or more of my contributions that the Annual contained. Even now, forty years later, it gives me pleasure to read it and be reminded of the annual Turkey Fair held at Attleborough in October of each year when about 5,000 birds were disposed of by auction, and many hundreds were driven in flocks through the streets, from the sale ground to the railway station for dispatch by passenger train to all parts of the country. Some were loaded loose into horse boxes; about 40 birds to each vehicle; and others loaded with five birds put into in special crates, provided by the auctioneers.

There was a reference to the natural freshwater springs that abound in the countryside around Narborough & Pentney station which were exploited commercially for producing the brown or winter variety of watercress. There were five watercress beds in all, each covering an area 40 yards long, and 20 yards wide. During the season, which extended from November to May, over 30 tons were conveyed by passenger train to London, Manchester and other markets. The cress was packed in peds or baskets each weighing two quarters 10lbs.

I told the readers about the rearing of pheasants and partridges in the Norfolk woodlands and countryside for the game shooting season which extends from September 1st to January 31st. Thousands of birds, the 'bags' of numerous shooting parties, were brought to our railway stations for conveyance to different parts of the country. The largest 'shoots' took place on the extensive estates situated in the vicinity of Brandon, Thetford and Harling Road stations and during the 1930 season approximately 200 tonnes of birds were dealt with at those stations. At the Didlington Hall Estate, near Brandon, one shooting party had included four reigning monarchs.

There was no apprehension that the birds would become extinct like the English bustard that used to live and breed in the same district because many thousands of pheasants and partridges eggs were brought in by passenger train every year from Great Missenden, Amersham and Emsworth for hatching purposes, and at North Walsham there was a game farm where 10,000 hen pheasants and 1,700 cock pheasants were penned annually for egg production and a total of over 200,000 eggs were produced each season.

Between April 15th and May 15th over 100,000 were dispatched from the farm in question, and practically all of them were carried by passenger train to all parts of the world. One basket of eggs was sent from North Walsham to the Kurren Valley, India, and despite a transit lasting over six weeks, over 60 per cent were hatched. About 20,000 eggs were dispatched to Scotland and others to regular customers in Germany, Poland, Sweden, South Africa and various State Game Departments in the United States, Canada, New Zealand and Ireland. To improve the strain of the birds many thousands were imported from the Continent. Six thousand pairs of partridges were brought over Hungary to North Walsham each winter and 100 live pheasants arrived at Norwich Thorpe station for an estate near

143

Wroxham, 40 came from Strasburg and 60 from a village five miles from Budapest.

I described the staple industry at Wells-next-the-Sea, which was whelk fishing. There was a fleet of eleven motor-boats, each equipped with 180 heavy iron whelk pots; baited with herrings or other fish and lowered into the sea eight miles from the land, with a heavy buoy fixed at each end to acquaint the fishermen of their position. The pots remained unattended until the following morning when they were hauled up, emptied, rebaited and again dropped into the sea, the boats returning to the shore on the morning tide. The majority of the whelks were then taken to a boiling house and cooked, afterwards being bagged and dispatched to various parts of the country. It was a lucrative business although extremely hazardous when the fishermen had to battle through rough seas only to find their pots had been swept away and lost.

It was much easier for those who dug up the lugworms with special flat tined forks at low tide from the wet sands on the East and West beaches. It was estimated that between 200,000 and 300,000 were dispatched by passenger train from Wells-on-Sea station during the months from September to March. They were packed in wooden boxes, well secured and of various sizes, each containing between 800 and 10,000 "wrigglers".

Sea anglers will be interested to learn they realised nine pence per hundred wholesale in 1931, which brought the cost of, say, 300,000 to £112. A friend tells me he recently paid almost one new penny each for his lugworms which on my calculation makes the retail price of 300,000 the dizzy figure of £3,000.

My daily routine in the office was disturbed one morning with a request to go up and see the 'Guvnor'. Mr Pettit told me our London Headquarters had arranged for one of their staff to show films to members of a sports club who were off to London on their annual outing by a special train departing from Great Yarmouth South Town station in the early hours of the next morning. He asked me to travel on the train and afterwards give my opinion of the experiment. I had the remainder of the

144

day off, officially to get my rest up, and Irene and I took the last train of the day to Great Yarmouth. It was Mr Pettit's idea I should take her with me. Let my report which I headed "Brighter Travel " tell you the rest of the story:

"A passenger on the 3.50am special train which conveyed members of the Falcon Sports Club from Yarmouth to the Metropolis on Saturday, September 26th 1931, awoke from a short doze and found the other occupants of the carriage had disappeared leaving their hats, bags and other paraphernalia behind them. Intrigued by their absence and sounds of sustained laughter coming from the rear of the train he walked along the brightly lighted corridor and found himself in a darkened coach. A light appeared by his side and he heard a voice exclaim "There's a seat in front. Will you come this way please?" He was escorted to a comfortably upholstered chair.

In front of him was an illuminated screen upon which the inimitable Charlie Chaplin, clad in evening dress and topper, was making futile but funny attempts to mount the stairs with the aid of an alpenstock, rucksack and rope, after a 'night out' and performing other mirth-provoking antics before eventually reaching the haven of his bedroom.

Then the lights went up on the interior of Brake Van number 5018. Its 60-foot length had the inviting appearance of a long narrow concert hall with seating accommodation for 25 persons. Chairs were arranged two on one side and one on the other side of a red carpeted centre aisle and in front was a Pathescope Cinema.

It was the latest phase in Brighter Travel introduced by the London and North Eastern Railway on long-distance excursion trains.

The Pathescope was in the charge of Mr W.G. Hayes, Passenger Manager's Department, King's Cross who had laughter provoking, sensational and educational films at his disposal. He gave five distinct performances, each lasting half an hour and when the train steamed into Liverpool Street station at 6.55am, 186 persons had thoroughly enjoyed a 'Show'.

145

The innovation seemed to strike the right note, it was acclaimed by the Falcon Sports Club party and should prove an incentive to party travel by rail.

This particular type of brake van, with its considerable floorspace and easy accessibility suggests other possibilities and I cannot help visualising it festooned into an impromptu dance hall with many bright young couples dancing to the strain of a fiddle or other musical instrument brought along by a member of their party whilst the guaranteed excursion train ploughs its way to some distant city or seaside resort."

Alas! The innovation did not strike any sort of chord in the Passenger Manager's office and I neither heard nor read of any further film shows on excursion trains. However, my vision of a 60-foot rail vehicle being converted for the entertainment of the young generation will, at long last, become reality, at a cost which would have staggered the railway management of the early 1930s. This will be the experimental super-train named the League Liner, which will be chartered to the Football League, and put into service in the year of our Lord 1973. A sixty-foot passenger coach has been converted for £15,000 into "The Kick off Disco", and another coach has been converted into a forty two seater with four colour television sets installed to play back video-taped matches. The total cost of the train will be £250,000.

A *Daily Mirror* reporter and photographer came to Norwich one day in 1932 to select six residents to give their comments on the question "Is modern life too rapid?" I do not know how they came to single me out and climb the stairs to my office to ask me the question and to take my photograph, subsequently published in the *Daily Mirror* with those of five other residents. Looking at it today, it seems a ludicrous question to have asked in that comparatively peaceful year. I liked best the comments of a young married girl who wrote-

"Speed and more speed. We are whisked from place to place with alarming rapidity. Machines to speed output are installed in our factories resulting in unemployment. We fray our nerves with everlasting bustle. Let us beware lest we are overtaken and destroyed by this thing called speed. What is life if we have no time to stand and stare?"

Could she have been building up in her mind a picture of the 'pile-ups' and 'snarl-ups' on our present-day motorways?

I can testify there was not much evidence of speeding on the roads in Norfolk in 1932 as I had the good fortune to have been released from the shackles of my office stool and given the job of calling on farmers throughout the whole of Norfolk in order to induce them to send their sugar beet to factories by rail. The position had not long been created and the senior clerk, Tich Eagle, who had been appointed to do the work, was taken seriously ill. I was selected because I was the only person in the office who could drive a car so my old Clyno had proved its worth after all.

Words cannot express my feelings as I drove a car, hired from a nearby garage, for the first time out of the station yard, with my colleagues watching enviously from the office windows under the clock. I was free to select any part of our delightful Norfolk countryside where sugar beet was being grown. I was in a new and happy world but there was a fly in the ointment, the farm dogs scared me. I started off by playing safe and calling at the front doors of the farmhouses but there was some delay before my knocks were answered. I could hear heavy bolts being drawn back; keys turned in the locks and doors being tugged open with difficulty by harassed looking occupants. I soon realised country people rarely used their front entrances. I went round to the back after that. At one farm there did not appear to be anybody at home, but I opened a low wicket gate and was on my way to the door to find out, when a big black dog bounded out of a kennel barking and snarling and came straight for me. It was a vicious looking beast, but I felt safe because I could see it was tethered to its kennel by a heavy chain. When the chain was at full stretch the onrush of the powerful dog was so violent that the chain snapped, and it was free. I froze to the spot where I was standing and then it happened, the dog stopped in its tracks as if by magic and slunk back into its kennel. To say I was relieved would be an understatement. I left the farm quicker than I went in and could only marvel at my escape from attack and can only conclude that the dog had done the same thing before and had been severely thrashed for it. I began to take stock of myself, as we say in Norfolk, to find out why I should be scared of other people's dogs, when I had an Airedale of my own and there was such a wonderful man-dog relationship between us.

It was a little black mongrel that gave me my 'complex' when I was ten years of age. It lived near to Carrie Hemming's house on Florence Road and every time it saw me walking by on the opposite path the hair on its back would bristle and it would growl, and bark and follow me for some distance, snapping at my heels as if I had no right to be there. It took no notice of the youngsters who played around it in the road nor to passers-by, except me, and its aversion was so obvious and persistent it disturbed me quite a bit, and I went in a different way when I saw it had been let out of its backyard. I made an exception one evening when I saw it with its master — a railway guard who knew me well — who was leaning over his front gate. I walked boldly past on the opposite path and gave him a cheery good-evening, he gave me a friendly salute in return, but his little beast growled, made a 'bee-line' for me and performed his usual snapping, to be peremptorily ordered back by his master. Why he should pick on me I could never understand.

So after recalling my alarming experience with the farm dog that broke away from its kennel, I was sitting in my car at the crossroads in Ashwellthorpe wondering which road I should take to get me to the residence of Lieutenant Colonel Daniels VC. I needed to call on him to canvas for his sugar beet to travel by rail. I went into the village blacksmith's shop to ask the way and noticed some parings from horses' hooves lying around. They took my mind back to a winter's night in France in 1916 when several of us soldiers were sitting around a hot tortoise stove in a Nissen hut. The subject of dogs cropped up and I related the story of the little black dog that used to scare me when I was young. That reminded another soldier of a friend of his who could never go for a walk in his village without being followed and barked at by dogs that took not the slightest notice of other people. He was advised to rub parings from horses' hooves round the bottoms of his trouser legs, which he did, and to his great relief, the dogs became friendly and followed him through the village like the Pied Piper of Hamelin. I decided to ask the blacksmith for some parings, and when I got back to my car, I rubbed the bottoms of my trousers with them and drove off to see the Colonel. He came out of his large house with two huge dogs at his heels as I turned into the courtyard where we got into conversation. All the while we were talking the dogs milled around me excitedly, and when they started jumping up as if I was their long-lost friend, the Colonel got exasperated at their unusual behaviour and peremptorily ordered them to get down. I told him they must have sensed my fondness for dogs!

When I got home my Airedale nearly went crazy with excitement until I changed my trousers. The parings had done the trick, they gave me a new ring of confidence and I always made sure there was a small piece in my 'turn-ups' as I boldly strode into farm premises where dogs were barking as a warning of my approach.

It might be difficult for fellow sufferers to try out the experiment as parings must be difficult to find nowadays, the smithy at Ashwellthorpe and many others have disappeared. My grandfather's blacksmith shop was in a tumble-down condition when I last saw it many years ago. When the old man retired, his nephew George Steele, took over the job and the day of reckoning for the old forge came when George died from lockjaw as the result of a kick from a horse.

I feel a tinge of sadness when I think of my mother's maiden name of Steele, which a succession of parish clerks have inscribed in the church register at Weeting for centuries past. It completely died out when George, the nephew, and my mother's brothers George and Fred, all passed away without leaving any children to carry on the family name.

It was several months before Tich Eagle was well enough to resume his duties as Sugar Beet Canvasser and I had, perforce, to go back into the office. My ambition was to become a canvasser, but I knew the chances were hopeless. Tich had at least twenty more years to go before he retired.

The opportunities for getting out of the office, even for a day, were few and far between, but I was recently reminded of the day I went to Carrow Works to obtain material for an article which I entitled "A Peep at Carrow Works". I was reminded of this when I read in the local press of the celebrations Reckitt and Colman Ltd. were making to celebrate the 150th anniversary of the founding of their business in 1823 at Stoke Holy Cross, a village four miles south of Norwich. I wish I had kept a copy of the article as I feel convinced the description of the activities at Carrow Works forty years previous, as seen through the eyes of an outsider, would have interested the firm in their 150th anniversary year*. All I have left is the short review by Whiffler, published in an *Eastern Evening News* in 1934 which made me 'puff my chest out'.

"Carrow works

NORWICH attains reflex publicity in the current issue of the *LNER Magazine* through an excellent article on Carrow Works by Mr F.G.G. Cobb. To give so adequate an idea of the industries and activities of Carrow in about a couple of pages of type all told argues no mean journalistic ability, and the description is assisted by illustrations, the most notable of which is a view of the Works from the air. Amongst the many details which emerge we are told that 21,000 'Blue-bags' per machine are produced per hour; that the sieves through which the ground mustard seeds are passed have 20,000 holes to the square inch; that mustard tins are filled, weighed and lidded at the rate of 3,000 per hour per machine and that 9,700 railway wagons were used for 20,350 tonnes of traffic during 1933."

Today rail traffic is practically non-existent and old railwaymen like myself sadly recall the time when two railway clerks were permanently housed in the firm's Transport Office to invoice out the large number of consignments dispatched each day, and the two railway engines belonging

---

The article has been located and is reproduced in the Appendix

to J. &. J. Colman Ltd., named Gamma and Delta, ribboned their way along the network of sidings, hauling railway wagons to and from the various depots and warehouses that were then connected to the rail network.

The road transport industry has completely displaced the railway and the once important station of Norwich Trowse has closed down, but what, I wonder, has become of Gamma and Delta and what inspired some erudite member of Carrow Works staff to give them names from the Greek alphabet.

When I left the office one morning in search of material for an article on the Norfolk cider industry, at the suggestion of Mr Pettit, my District Manager, I little realised the visit to William Gaymer and Son, Attleborough, would turn out to be the most memorable of many I was to make on people in all walks of life. I was received by Mr William Chapman Gaymer, Managing Director, with his usual buoyant, busi-ness-like manner. I reminded him we had met previously at Bawdsey in March 1916 when he, as Orderly Officer of the Day, bade "good luck" and "goodbye" to my draft of Norfolk's which was leaving for service overseas. It seemed to add something to our meeting as he was keenly interested in the 2/4th Norfolk's Old Comrades Association and was its first president. "You must speak to father;" he said and took me to see an active gentleman of 91 years of age who still attended at his office regularly every morning.

He was the founder of the thriving business which he had started years before in the village of Banham where he made cider from apples grown in his own extensive orchards.

As long as I can remember the railways of Great Britain have had brickbats hurled at them and it was refreshing to hear Mr Gaymer speak appreciatively of them. He told me his firm was unique throughout the country as it was the only one that used the railways exclusively for the move-ment of their traffic in and out of the Works. There was abundant evidence at Attleborough station to confirm this. The Class 2 Station Master was constantly in touch with Gaymer's Transport Manager, Maynard Clark. There were thirteen clerks in the Goods Office and one clerk in the

Parcels Office dealing with nothing but Gaymer's traffic. A railway checker worked full-time inside the Works and a railway engine with engine driver and fireman plus two shunters and their shunt horses were also needed to deal with the daily influx of loaded wagons. The output of cider averaged forty wagons a day in the summer months when the thirsts of the populace were at their maximum. In the apple season as many as thirty wagons a day were shunted into the works mainly from the Wisbech district.

Mr Gaymer passed me on to his Chief Clerk, Mr Harrison, a tremendous character, with instructions that he should take me out to lunch. The latter charged my glass with sparkling cider and gave me the facts I needed. After a tour of the works he took me to the local Inn where we drank some liqueurs whilst waiting for lunch to be served. I soon realised I was no drinker as I walked unsteadily to the dining table where I was served with the thickest and most delicious steak I have ever tasted. I could only remember feeling like it on two previous occasions. Once when young Chettleburgh and I forsook the dreary streets of wartime Peterborough in December 1914 for the bright lights of a pub, and drank four glasses of port each, at threepence a glass, and the second time when we celebrated our departure from Hinges for Italy in champagne.

I was scared that my condition might deteriorate and I struggled hard to throw off the effects of the mixed drinks. Mr Harrison did not appear to have noticed anything amiss with me, but I had a feeling he was eyeing me quizzically to see how I was standing up to his firm's hospitality. Fortunately, I got no worse, but it was a great relief when I said goodbye to him at Attleborough station and sank into a seat on the train which took me back to Norwich Thorpe station.

The article on the cider industry duly appeared in print and for many years afterwards a box of choice apples from Mr Gaymer was delivered to our house at Christmas time; which was a nice way of reminding me of a great day and a great man.

Later in my career I had cause to remember Mr Gaymer's remarks to me about his firm being the only one in the country to use rail exclusively. I was closely connected with political and domestic events which led to the complete transfer of Gaymer's traffic to road transport and to the closure of Attleborough goods station; a story which will be unfolded in later pages of this book.

The story of my humble passage through life may seem insignificant compared with the paths of golden opportunities and gifted achievements of men like Harold Macmillan and Malcolm Muggeridge who have just published their autobiographies but at least I have, in my own way, experienced the same kind of thrills and emotions as they must have had when delving into the past. I agree, categorically, with Malcolm Muggeridge when he told a reporter "The best thing about autobiography is it forces you to think about your life, a thing we all tend to avoid doing. It is odd how things viewed from old age dwindle into their correct prospective. You surprise yourself how trivial were the things that caused great anguish… and how those things are not important in comparison with the great inevitable force which determines that you do indeed meet the right person at the right time." Those remarks appeared in the *Daily Mail* of August 4th 1973, and they correspond exactly with my own near matrimonial exploits from which the same "great inevitable force" guided my step to the right girl who would share my future. We started our married life the same year Mr Pettit came to Norwich and he, like Irene, made a great impact on my life.

It was the practice at Headquarter Offices for the Manager to discuss all matters with the Chief Clerk, or Chiefs of Sections, which presented no opportunities or occasions for other members of the office staff to be called into the presence of our District Officer. When Mr Hall reigned supreme it was a great relief to us young members of the staff, as we got butterflies at the thought of being sent to face his steely blue eyes. To the clerical workers of today, protected as they are by their Unions and Office Councils, it may seem a strange weakness, but let them dwell on the case of the Chief Clerk at a station, who was brought in to fill a vacancy in our office which was created by the promotion of the Chief Clerk to Station Master at Great Yarmouth. We all thought at long last there would be a chain of promotions within the office, but Mr Hall fancied the nice looking station clerk and appointed him to take charge of the General section. Not many months later he was summoned to the sanctum sanctorum and it was not difficult to guess what had transpired. He came back to his table, sat down and wept. It was a shock to see a grown man so distressed. In fairness to him he had no experience of District Office work and was sent back to a station.

It was all so different when Mr Pettit took over as District Goods and Passenger Manager. It was obvious he wanted to keep in touch with the younger members of his staff, and he encouraged anything that would bring all his personal staff together socially; office dinners, outings and the formation of a cricket team, which was his own suggestion and to which he gave a good financial boost to get it going.

I always got the task of organising the new projects. I enjoyed doing this as it was a change from routine office work. Mr Pettit always accompanied us to cricket matches which we arranged on Saturday afternoons with the District Office staffs in London, Cambridge and Ipswich, meeting the teams at places equidistant. He was generous with free rail passes for the whole party which included wives and sweethearts.

When he was Chairman-Elect of the Literary and Debating Society, he asked me to take over the Secretaryship. We were both elected at the next General Meeting and I soon realised it was marvellous opportunity for a budding speaker to get a platform.

It was sometime before I could pluck up enough courage to stand up and speak and then I had written it all out in longhand in case I should dry up with fright. The morning after, Mr Pettit congratulated me and thereon gave me such encouragement that I was soon debating from the platform.

When Mr Pettit took part in a debate he would ask me to think of some points he could make use of. I thought it was an honour to be asked even though it took me hours preparing them at home; which he knew nothing about. He thought I had time to do it in office hours. I wonder if that sort of unpaid blind loyalty exists today. I was amply rewarded when I sat in the body of the hall, with Irene beside me, listening to him talking about what was literally my own work.

One morning he asked me how I thought he could make use of two toy railway engines he had just bought in the City to advertise the evening excursions for theatre goers which he had arranged from Norwich to Liverpool Street. It was nothing to do with my own clerical work, but I was past being surprised at anything he asked me to do.

Two sandwich-board men were being hired to parade the streets of Norwich displaying posters and distributing handbills. It was decided that they were to be dressed up in morning coats and tall hats and a toy engine was to be fixed on top of each topper. I took the two engines home and cut out two tin shapes resembling the steam puffing from the funnel of a moving engine; painted them white and printed in black on both sides 'LONDON — 6/6d'. I thought the scheme would belittle the prestige of the railways as the sandwich men (one was tall and the other short) looked 'down at heel' and in no way resembled theatre patrons, but I kept my opinion to myself.

The press published a photograph of them which was an additional advertisement and the excursions turned out to be popular and a financial success. Fancy going from Norwich to London and back by rail for 32½ new pence. Evening excursions were introduced from Norwich to Great Yarmouth at nine pence return and were also successful.

It was a sad moment for me when I first heard of Mr Pettit's appointment as Chief of LNER Police on the retirement of Major Chauncy. He had been a good boss and I owed much to him, not from a financial angle as he had no power to create promotions, but from the confidence and encouragement he gave me. When I

155

MR. R. R. PETTIT

WE have pleasure in announcing that MR. R. R. PETTIT, District Goods and Passenger Manager, Norwich, will succeed Major A. C. Chatney as Chief of Police, Southern Area.

Mr. Pettit has been a popular district officer at the capital of East Anglia. He returns to the Police Department after 15 years' absence. During that time he has occupied the positions of Chief Clerk to the London Divisional Com-

Mr. R. R. Pettit

mercial Superintendent, Joint Assistant to the London District Passenger Manager, Assistant District Passenger Manager (London), followed by the Norwich appointment as from May, 1929.

Much of his earlier experience was drawn from the traffic departments, in which he performed clerical duties at stations and at headquarters for 12 years. In 1904 he entered the Police Department at Liverpool Street as Chief Clerk, eventually being promoted to Assistant to the Chief of Police with the rank of Superintendent. He has now won his way through to the Chief's chair—a chair of high responsibility—and many of those who know his capabilities and have helped him on the upward path will no doubt share in the prediction that the affairs of the department will continue to be efficiently administered.

London & North Eastern Railway Magazine
January 1933

congratulated him, he enquired if I would like to work in London and told me to put in for any position that might be advertised later. In due time a third class clerical post at Police Headquarters, Liverpool Street station was advertised, and I applied for it. The day before I went to London for an interview my Chief Clerk sent for me and in a friendly chat told me not to be disappointed if I did not get the job. I sensed he had heard something.

When my train was slowing down outside Liverpool Street station, I glanced out from the carriage window at a smoke begrimed old house overlooking a network of railway lines and my heart sank when I realised that there was where I would have to spend my working days if I was selected. I thought of my interesting view from the windows of our office at Thorpe station, of the merry antics of my colleagues, the house and garden Irene and I had spent long years to bring up to our idea of paradise and the recreational facilities we were enjoying. All this to give up for a rise of three shillings and ten pence a week plus three shillings and ten pence a week London allowance. At the interview Mr Pettit chatted only about Norwich and when it was over he phoned the Manager of the Staff Canteen to provide me with the best lunch possible at his expense. What a fine boss he had been. I was very relieved when I heard in due course the job had been given to Dick Woodward from Nottingham, my senior in service.

Sometime later Mr Pettit came to Norwich and stayed overnight. He spent most of the evening watching us play badminton in the Ailwyn Hall. Irene and I were there and then I told him how I was glad I did not get the position as the third class clerk in his office. He was delighted to hear it and relieved too as he had been under the impression, ever since the interview, I was sadly disappointed. 'All's well that ends well.'

I had never heard of Dick Woodward until he got the job in the Police Department. He did not stay long but re-joined the Commercial Department in the London District Goods Manager's office and it was twenty years later when we found we had much in common. He was then Head of

Development, Ipswich district and I was his opposite number in the Norwich district. We attended monthly meetings at London HQ and got to know each other best when we chummed up on a three-day tour of Northern Ireland which we attended, with other Heads of Development from Headquarter Offices throughout Great Britain, at the invitation of the Ulster Tourist Board.

We were escorted by coach to all places of interest to tourists, and at the numerous hotels we inspected the Managers showed us their well-stocked cellars and invited us to choose our drinks. We received VIP treatment throughout the whole tour; and were wined and dined with high dignitaries. We were filled with praise for the Ulster Tourist Board and happy and ready to admit that life on the railway had its compensations.

Mr H.C. Statham, the new District Goods and Passenger Manager carried on where Mr Pettit left off. He was not so free and easy in conversation but that was his nature and not a fault. He started well by inviting the members of his staff, and their wives, to spend an evening on his private tennis court and both he and Mrs Statham joined in everything that was going on, tennis and cricket in the summer, badminton and debating in the winter. In the office he expressed concern I had been in the same grade for so many years and urged me to apply for positions in other districts. He gave me a good recommendation every time I went for an interview but the man on the spot got the job every time.

Chapter 14 — LNER and Mr Wilson

It was a welcome change when I was taken off my routine office duties and went to Cambridge by train two or three times a week. The Road Traffic Act of 1930 laid down that Coach Operators must submit applications for licences to run Stage Coach, Express Services and Excursions and Tours to the Traffic Commissioner, who for the eastern region was Sir Haveland Hiley, with offices at Cambridge. I went there to take copies of applications from Coach Operators which could adversely affect railway carryings, so that the railway authorities could oppose them at subsequent Traffic Court Hearings if considered desirable. At the appointed day a junior clerk had gone to Cambridge, but he had upset a member of the Traffic Commissioner's staff and a letter had been received by our District Officer requesting him not to send the offending clerk to Cambridge again, and that is how I came into the picture. I was diplomacy personified and got on well with the offending clerk but nearly unwittingly landed myself into worse trouble one morning when I had been given the use of an office on a different floor level than usual. You could not tell the difference between one floor and another, or one loo from another for that matter, as I found out to my dismay when I dashed into what I thought was the "Gents" on the landing and was sitting comfortably when I heard young ladies chatting on the other side of my closet door. I was petrified and literally glued to my seat until I was certain that they had gone. I rushed out without meeting a soul for which I was truly thankful.

I usually had about three hours to spare before catching my train back to Norwich and after lunch I would stroll through the Colleges and the Backs; swim in a bathing pool or paddle a hired canoe on the River Cam. I meandered through some of the loveliest parts of Cambridge, where dragonflies darted in the sunlight and young men with their bright young ladies floated by in punts and rowing boats or languished under the shade of overhanging trees. It was a splendid way for a railwayman to earn his living!

As years rolled by, memory has become a kaleidoscope of events I find difficult to place in an exact yearly order. It was, I think, sometime in 1934 that I walked along the corridor to the District Operating Superintendent's office to confer with Bob Greenwood, who worked closely with me in our joint efforts to trace the whereabouts of loaded wagons that were missing or delayed in transit. The railways were zealous in their efforts to maintain next morning deliveries, there were daily services to and from the principal towns and cities, London, Manchester, and Liverpool for example, and the phones would soon start ringing if supplies for industry, trades and shops did not arrive the morning after dispatch.

I met Mr F.C. Wilson, the District Superintendent in the General Office. He had just been notified that one of his clerks, Harold Robinson, son of the Station Master at Lowestoft Central, had been appointed to the Train Section in the office of the Superintendent of the Line, at Liverpool Street.

"How would you like to work in the operating department?" he asked me. The question was quite unpremeditated as it was mere chance that we should both be in his General Office at the same time, but that was F.C. Wilson all over. His forthrightness and appearance earned him the nickname of Mussolini when he came to Norwich as Station Master in the early 1920s, having previously been Assistant Station Master at Liverpool Street. He demonstrated his ability as a man of action and a practical railwayman at the time of the general strike in 1926 when he worked the Norwich Yard signal box with the only member of the outside staff to stay on duty. Their joint action and the help of bowler-hatted volunteers from the general public, who acted as engine drivers, firemen, guards and porters, made it possible for trains to run in and out of Norwich Thorpe station. The loyal signalman stuck to his

160

duties and his principles throughout the whole of the strike and, although he was sent to Coventry by his fellow workers almost indefinitely afterwards, he avoided the large lump of coal that 'accidentally' fell from the tender of an engine as he was passing. His strong will and faith in God enabled him to ride the tempestuous storms of ill feeling. He was a man of character and the father of my close boyhood friend, George.

F.C. Wilson's progress was meteoric. He was appointed Station Master at Liverpool Street and, not many years afterwards, back again in Norwich as District Superintendent. Four years later he was District Superintendent, Stratford, the Senior District in the Eastern Region.

While he was at Norwich, he made an after-dinner speech which hit the headlines in the *Eastern Daily Press* the next morning. A caption blazoned the words:

"NORWICH IS LIVING ON THE PAST"

The purpose of this speech was the city authorities were "behind the times" and paying more attention to their ancient buildings than to the tremendous potential for development. 'F.C.' saw its great future as a large and important inland port. The river Yare could be dredged so that large ocean-going ships could ply direct from the Continent to Norwich, where specially constructed docks could be built at which their cargoes could be discharged, instead of at Great Yarmouth, thus avoiding the additional handling and the transport by rail or road to Norwich. The inevitable letters of protest appeared in the press. He smiled when they were mentioned to him in conversation. He had made his point and characteristically stuck to it.

He had been at Stratford for about a year when Irene and I went to Shanklin, Isle of Wight, for our fortnight's annual holiday. The first afternoon we strolled along the water's edge on Hope Beach and were attracted by two people waving and beckoning to us from across the beach. As we got nearer and they took off their sunglasses, we realised it was Mr and Mrs Wilson who, too, had just arrived to take possession of their hired beach hut. They made us extremely welcome and we stayed for a cup of tea, becoming more and more absorbed in each other's experiences since they left Norwich. In the evening we went to community singing which set the seal on our friendships for the whole of the next fortnight. I sang as lustily as if I was swinging along on a route march with the boys of the 2/4th Norfolk's and F.C. held forth with a gusto that stripped him of the cares of his high office. We were in real holiday mood and the difference in our ages did not seem to matter. We sang community songs when seated in our deck chairs on the beach, when promenading along the Esplanade and on coach tours, but we found time to chat while our wives followed behind, intent upon enjoying each other's company.

Mr Wilson told me about his first Station Master's job at Shippea Hill where he was also the village postmaster. The post office was run from the booking office. It was a busy place and he was so popular with the farmers and other rail users, the presents they gave him at Christmas time would have filled a railway truck.

He had not been Station Master at Liverpool Street long before he issued instructions that a certain train should be worked into a particular platform and the signalman said it could not be done. The last thing a member of his staff should have done was to refuse to obey his orders and just before the train was due F.C. went to the signal box and confronted the signalman who stuck to his opinion. Mr Wilson then took command, he worked the levers and the train steamed into the required platform.

Those who have worked with him and knew his reputation could have no illusions about what transpired in the signal box after that practical demonstration. The dialogue ended when the signalman told him he was used to being spoken to by Station Masters with kid gloves on to which F.C. retorted "You'll find I shall be wearing mailed gauntlets the next time I come into this box if my instructions are not carried out".

I discovered the real man during that holiday in Shanklin and what I saw and heard I greatly admired. Crowds seem to stimulate his inborn instinct and I can imagine him in his glory when Liverpool Street station was teeming with passengers and something had gone wrong on the operating side. He would lead us through waiting crowds to good seats in restaurants for morning coffee, and when we arrived late for a concert on the Pier and people thronged the entrance, we followed behind him and found ourselves comfortably ensconced in front row seats long before those at the back had settled in. When I chaffed him about his seeming boldness, he said it was a question of mind over matter and instanced an occasion when, dressed in morning suit and topper and accompanied by Mrs Wilson, he went off to watch an important civic procession in the City of London and spotted the Lord Mayor and Lady Mayoress with important officials and their ladies sitting on a raised balcony high over the heads of the crowd. "Come on, my dear," he said to his wife "we are going to sit up there." A uniformed attendant stopped him at the entrance and said, "You cannot be admitted without a ticket, Sir." F.C. took a five pound note from his wallet, folded it carefully and handed to the man. "Will this ticket do?" he said. They were escorted to seats next to the Lord Mayor.

He was at the top of his form when we all met by arrangement at Shanklin station on the morning of our departure for home.

It was August Bank Holiday Saturday, the busiest day of the year for the railways. Crowds were invading the station circulating area and flocking on to the platform, intent on catching their train. I could see something was happening to F.C. as he regarded the animated scene with the experienced eyes of a District Operating Superintendent. He spotted the Station Master in the distance and ploughed his way purposefully past fathers struggling with heavy suitcases, mothers anxiously watching their children, passengers standing and others jockeying for position where they could make a dash for seats on the train which they knew would be well filled with passengers who had got on at Ventnor, the starting point. We watched Mr Wilson as he kept this Station Master in conversation until the train came in, then he beckoned to us and we were all ushered into a first-class compartment; the door of which the Station

Master had opened with his square headed key. I am sure the gracious official never dreamt Irene and myself were travelling with third class free passes. He locked the door at F.C.'s request and we sat back to enjoy a quiet, undisturbed journey to Ryde.

Mr. F. C. Wilson, M.B.E.

DESCRIBED by the National Press as "the man who kept the trains running in and out of Liverpool Street Station during the 1940-41 blitz," MR. F. C. WILSON, M.B.E., district superintendent, Stratford, retired on December 21, 1944.

Mr. Wilson entered the service of the Great Eastern Railway over 50 years ago as a junior clerk at Saffron Walden. His first appointment as stationmaster was in his home county of Norfolk. In 1915 he was assistant stationmaster at Liverpool Street, and subsequently he became stationmaster there, then district superintendent at Norwich, and in October, 1933, district superintendent at Stratford. His many interests included Life Governorship of numerous hospitals. He was also an Hon. Life Member of the British Red Cross and a Serving Brother in the Order of St. John of Jerusalem.

A number of presentations were made by various sections of the staff to mark Mr. Wilson's retirement. At Bishopsgate Goods Agent's Office, on December 18, the Operating and Cartage staffs presented a silver cigarette case, suitably inscribed, and a Ronson lighter; the following day he received a silver salver from the officers of the Superintendent's Eastern Section, and on December 20 a wireless set from his own personal staff. The stationmasters, yardmasters, agents and outside staff of the Stratford district presented Mr. Wilson with a granddaughter clock. Many speeches of respect and affection were made.

London & North Eastern Railway Magazine January 1945

There was the same frantic rush at Portsmouth as passengers made their way from the Isle of Wight boat to the waiting train. F.C. again took command and insisted that Irene and I should keep with them. He then led us to an empty first-class compartment and framed himself in the window of the door ready to point to the figure '1' on the outside of the door should anybody have ideas about coming in. He was in high spirits and turned to remark to us in jest "I'll tell them one of you has measles, that'll keep them out". A porter looked in and enquired if we were all first-class passengers and, to my great relief, F.C. answered "Yes", so loudly and so convincingly, he went on his way and so did the train which was non-corridor and non-stop to Waterloo. There would be an uproar nowadays if passengers had to travel so far and at such inconvenience without a convenience.

I never saw him again but strange to relate my interest in him was rekindled in recent months when I read, in a book by G.F. Fiennes, entitled "I tried to run a railway", that the writer, who was familiarly known to railwaymen as Gerry Fiennes, took over the position of District Superintendent, Stratford on the retirement of "Freddie C. 'Musso' Wilson" at the end of 1944.

So, the name of Mussolini had stuck to him right up to the time of his retirement. The book is a 'must' for railwaymen of my generation. It reveals, among so many intimate facts in his career, the poor salaries the railway masters paid their District Officers. It seems inconceivable the District Superintendent of the largest district on the LNER, with a staff of about 10,000, should receive only £800 per annum which was the salary of the 2nd class clerk not many years later.

The powerful story of the rise of Gerry Fiennes from a "timetable clerk" (his definition) to Chairman and General Manager of the Eastern Region of British Railways makes me realise what a tiny cog in the wheel I was and never a railwayman in the true sense of the word. Timing and diagramming left me cold; engines never stirred my emotions, buck-eye couplings still remain a mystery, and trains were for filling with passengers, or freight, by my efforts and those of my colleagues in the Commercial department.

I was a commercial man to the core and glad I did not follow up Mr Wilson's suggestion and apply for Harold Robinson's job when he was promoted to Liverpool Street. We were shocked and saddened when we heard that he had died at a comparatively early age. He had reached the highest position on the Eastern Region in his special sphere and we wondered if the stress and strain of his high of office had contributed to his early demise. What would have happened if he had remained in the modest calm of the Norwich District Superintendent's office? It was a futile speculation because it is an acknowledged truism that a railwayman must move from his home district if he wants to advance and it was inevitable he should follow the path chosen him by his Destiny.

Chapter 15
Out and About With LNER

It was round about the year 1935 when we had our holiday with the Wilsons at Shanklin and the front page of the *Daily Mail* had become the shop window of the nation. Firms were queueing to take the whole page to advertise their products. The staggering price was £1,000 for one day's insertion. When our train left Norwich en route to Shanklin I was attracted by a front page advertisement in my *Daily Mail* for Julysia Hair Cream in which the makers offered a first prize of a ten horsepower Morris motor car to the purchaser of a bottle of their hair cream if he found the largest number of mistakes in a pen and ink sketch; a three and a half horse-power Norton motorcycle for the second largest number, and numerous money prizes for the runners-up. I thought it would while away many an otherwise idle hour when sitting in a deck chair on beach, but my plans went awry when we met the Wilsons, and I had neither the time nor the inclination to bother about competitions.

I had won £5 in a similar sort of competition run by the makers of Toffee Rex and fancied my chances of winning again so, when the holiday was over, I spent many hours looking at the picture for such things as missing fingers and when I finally posted a bulky envelope it contained 1,770 detailed errors. I won the second prize of a three and a half horsepower Norton motorcycle, and was left wondering how many mistakes the winner of the Morris Ten car could have found in the sketch which measured about seven inches square. I went off to London by train to fetch it; taxed and insured it, thinking it really nice to take Irene out 'pillion', but I never recaptured the thrills of my early motorcycling days after the comforts of my old Clyno, so I sold it and bought Irene a fur coat, which gave us both real pleasure, she, when she wore it, and me, when I took her out in it.

The time I spent canvassing when Tich Eagle was ill, the odd occasions I went out to find material for the *LNER Magazine* and the trips to the Traffic Commissioners, Cambridge unsettled me in the office, and my hopes of becoming a canvasser brightened when the LNER decided to appoint two canvassers to each commercial district. They would be graded 4th class, be provided with a car and cover rural areas.

Although it would not mean promotion, as I had been in the same grade since 1919, I longed for a company car, the open road and freedom to use my initiative in persuading farmers and traders to use rail transport. I applied for one Norwich position and knew I would have the backing of my District Manager and Chief Clerk. The interviews were held on a regional basis, all applicants being ordered to Liverpool Street Headquarters to appear before a selection panel of HQ staff. I went to see Herbert Duncan, my tailor in St Giles Street, who rigged me up with an expensive overcoat and bowler hat. I wanted to leave nothing to chance in my efforts to impress. I'm convinced it was the spats that lost me the job! I can feel the interviewers looking down at them as I walked across the office floor and could almost hear them saying "Fancy going into a pub on the Norwich cattle market and talking to a cattle dealer with spats on." I was dismayed when the sad news came through that I had been passed over and my office colleagues openly expressed their indignation. I had overdone the sartorial act.

Not many days later fortune smiled on me, I was given a duty travelling pass and freedom of the Norwich district. The LNER had got itself into a pickle with wagon shortages. They had not been building new stock quickly enough to keep pace with the large number of condemned wagons and the growing pile of "cripples" awaiting repair. There was widespread difficulty all over the region in meeting wagon requirements and the position was likely to be aggravated when the new season's grain commenced to be moved. The sugar beet season was also in the offing when the LNER could expect to carry around about 1,000,000 tonnes to beet factories. My job was to speed up the turnaround of wagons by inspecting station yards and sidings, and, if necessary, to make personal calls on merchants and traders to seek their co-operation by clearing their wagons more quickly.

Some days I took my bicycle on the train and rode through peaceful country lanes to the next station and I even prevailed upon the Company to pay me one shilling and six pence a day for the hire of the cycle. Other days I would spend my meal hours and the waiting time between trains watching the waves and inhaling refreshing ozone at Cromer, Great Yarmouth, Lowestoft and other Norfolk resorts. Sometimes I would join one or other of the canvassers in their cars so we could 'hunt in pairs'. It was great fun and the next best thing to canvassing. It involved no great effort, especially in the slack season when you've plenty of wagons standing idle. I had been "wagon chasing" for about two years when our headquarters at Liverpool Street found out I was still doing the job and they immediately told my District Goods and Passenger Manager, in no uncertain manner, I should have been taken off the work months before.

Looking back is like turning over the pages of the book, each event seems to fit smoothly into the pattern of my life. There was a new position created by the DG & PM, Ipswich which appeared on the Vacancy List pinned on our noticeboard the same morning I returned to my desk saddened by the thought I might have to remain an indoor clerk for the rest of my career. It was for a 4th class passenger canvasser for an experimental period of six months after which time the continuance of the position would depend on results achieved.

It was an opportunity for me to realise my ambition to become a railway representative even though it did not mean promotion for me. Irene and I would have to leave our much loved house and garden which we had worked hard on for ten years, we would miss our families, our friends, the tennis club and our social activities but as Irene said she would go where I went so I applied and was duly appointed.

Our garden at Lime Tree Avenue

We were delighted when my mother and sisters decided to buy our house in Lime Tree Avenue and move from the stuffy atmosphere of their terraced house in Beatrice Road, to the heights of Norwich where they could sit or work in the garden and smell the fresh air wafting over from the coast. I was thrilled when I commenced work in the District Office at Ipswich in August 1937 and found myself left to take my own course of action to discover what potential passenger traffic lay untapped in the district which embraced the whole of Suffolk and parts of Essex as far as Ingatestone.

I spent the first fortnight in Ipswich distributing scales of parcels charges to shops and factories pointing out it was cheaper to send by rail than by post. It may have been a coincidence and nothing at all do with my initiative but there was a large increase in outwards parcel traffic from Ipswich station during my six months probationary period compared with the same period the previous year, but the figures looked impressive in my report and may have helped to influence Headquarters to make the position permanent. I visited schools, secretaries of women's organisations, works outings and football clubs to extol the advantage of special trains for large parties and reduced fares for smaller parties. It was the proudest moment of my life when I stood on Liverpool Street station platform and saw 650 schoolchildren and their teachers pour out of my very first train. It was all my own work and the forerunner of many others, the majority of which were to Windsor and Eton station, where the parties embarked on Salter Bros.

steamers for trips down the River Thames to Maidenhead and Hampton Court.

There was never a dull moment. When the outing season was over, I might spend a day with the Transport Manager at Hoffmans, Cromptons or Marconi's at Chelmsford; or at Courtaulds or Crittalls at Braintree. Another day I could be having morning coffee near Willi Lott's cottage in Constable's country or stopping to gaze for the first time at the huge bells hanging in a cage in the churchyard at East Bergholt. There was a changing panorama of boat building at Mersea; sprats being landed at Brightlingsea, and women sitting at their open front doors peeling shrimps. At the Xylonite Works at Brantham, matches and pipes had to be left at the entrance by visitors and a pungent smell invaded the lungs. This was only exceeded in intensity by the smell of spices when I called at a pepper mill a few hundred yards distant; a smell which remained in my nose for days afterwards. There were the seaside resorts from Maldon in Essex to Southwold in Suffolk where at the Adnams Brewery I was given a glass of beer by a gentlemanly octogenarian clerk whose good looks and waxen complexion any woman would have been proud to possess.

For good measure I viewed the delightful country around Lavenham with its beautiful church and lovely old houses; Long Melford and Kersey. To my shame I had never heard of Kersey village until I came across it unexpectedly when I called to see a Major who resided at the top of the hill. I stood motionless with amazement as I looked down on a narrow street with its well-preserved mediaeval houses on either side. It was just like stepping into the past. There was not a movement anywhere save some ducks waddling in a shallow ford at the far end of the street. I walked through the street twice for an extra antiquarian feast.

At Long Melford I saw a new 1937 Austin 7 Ruby Saloon, in my favourite colour of blue, in the window of a motor engineers' shop and went in to ask the price. It was £127. Just the thing I thought, for Irene and me to slip over to Norwich at weekends. I could afford to pay one shilling and three pence a gallon for petrol because I had given up smoking before I left Norwich and it would be an added incentive not to start again if I bought petrol for the enjoyment of my family instead of cigarettes for my destruction. The car was still in the window the next time I went to Long Melford and the price was the same. I pointed out to the salesman I could get the next year's model at that price at the motor show being held at Earls Court and persuaded him to let me have it for £115, which included new number plates and a full tank of petrol. The Ruby Saloon turned out to be as invaluable an investment as my old Clyno had been as I was given permission to use it for my own work and it was the forerunner of a continuity of cars throughout my life.

I attended all Thornton & Hobson's sales of pedigree cattle and pigs. These attracted influential buyers from all parts of the country and I sat beside the auctioneer's clerk to deal with rail transport enquiries and arrangements. I went with Frank Saward, the cattle canvasser for the Ipswich district, to the annual sales of lambs which took place in July of each year. At Barnham, for example, over 6,000 were auctioned in a field at the back of the village pub, and at Sutton, near Melton in the heart of Suffolk, where sales had been held for well over a hundred and twenty years, 6,000 to 7,000 were on offer. Frank and I were kept busy at Diss when we secured 617 wagon loads for rail movement for a total of between 17,000 and 18,000 lambs. They were mainly Suffolk, Southdown or crossbreds. It is estimated there were at least 60,000 auctioned at the ten principal markets in the Ipswich district. Where have all the lambs gone?

Chapter 16 — World War II

Irene and I settled down very well. We bought a house in Ipswich when my position was made permanent; we joined a tennis club and when I was unable to find a badminton club, I found a suitable church hall and formed a club from the office staff and their ladies.

The one disappointment was that we had not been able to hear the patter of tiny feet in our happy home. Our doctor had been consulted and friends gave us plenty of advice. At badminton Irene was told about a country parson who went to bed with a poke hat on and became a father. I had not got a poke hat so that advice came to naught. We were told to tie a stone with a hole in it to the garden gate. We found one at the seaside and for a joke tied it on the back gate. When we reported a lack of success, we were told the reason for the failure was that we should have tied one on to the front gate as well to keep the luck in. This we did and, after twelve years of married life, in 1940, Janette, a baby girl of nine pounds four ounces, brought joy that completed our happiness.

I was proud of Irene on the night she was in bed awaiting the happy event. Her mother and myself were in the bedroom keeping her company, and at that point the sirens went. Almost immediately the drone of German bombers was heard and then the whining of bombs as they hurtled to the ground. We seemed to be rising up to meet them, until we heard the deafening crashes, and the house shuddered. Irene was not the least disturbed and quickly allayed my feelings of alarm for her well-being when she smiled at me sweetly and said "I'm alright. I have got something better to think about". She was wonderful throughout the night when a child was born and three souls went to heaven, victim of Hitler's bombs.

The war had changed the pattern of our lives, the man-in-the-street was an air raid warden, a special constable or a Home Guard. We were under the stern control of the DORA (the Defence of the Realm Act), windows had to be blacked out and the all too frequent nerve chilling warning whine of the sirens sent us hurrying into the air raid shelters we had dug in our gardens.

Railways had become an integral part of the war machine, tanks, guns and troops took preference over normal traffic and there were posters everywhere enjoining travelling public to ask themselves the question "Is your journey really necessary?" Reduced fare facilities and party travel were withdrawn, and my passenger canvassing activities came to an end. I was given a desk in the Chief Clerk's office to deal with war emergencies. Nobody had any idea what might happen, and nothing did during the many hours I spent each day and on Sundays waiting for something to turn up. What actually turned up for me was another welcome release from the office chair. This time entirely due to me having changed my Austin Ruby saloon for a new Standard Eight which cost £139. It proved to be as lucky and invaluable an investment as my old Clyno had been because the car, and myself as driver, were loaned to C. Bloomfield Smith, the District Engineer. He had found the need for a car and a driver to speed him to the scenes of enemy actions against railway installations, and for other projects that had greatly increased as a result of the war.

C.B. Smith had joined the railway from an outside company rather late in his career and because of this he had one fine attribute which was lacking in many of the officers who started their careers on the railway, he treated his staff as equal and they respected him for it. We got on well together, fraternising at each other's houses and playing tennis on his private tennis court.

The highlights of our daily jaunts were frequent visits to the naval base at Parkeston Quay and Harwich where the Naval authorities constantly needed to consult him about structural alterations to railway property for defence purposes and such staff amenities as a new chapel, cinema, messrooms and the like. I was there when our soldiers landed from Dunkirk. It was a sad and unforgettable sight. The poor fellows looked tired, dejected, hungry and badly in need of sleep and a refreshing wash.

They were very jittery about spies at Harwich. C.B. had been invited by an officer to a working lunch at a hotel and after he had left the car on Harwich Quay, I realised I did not know where I had to pick him up again. I parked the car and was about to walk to a restaurant for my lunch when I stopped a workman who was passing, explained what had happened, and asked him what hotel he thought they would be lunching at. There were very few in wartime Harwich and his choice was the correct one. Several days later my neighbour, who was an Inspector in the Special Constabulary, popped his head over the garden fence and informed me the police had been asking him questions about me. The Harwich Police had sent them a report (with my car number) which, in effect, stated that a suspicious character had been asking questions on the Quay which could lead to information of military value being passed to the enemy. How the man I spoke to came to that conclusion, it is difficult to comprehend, however, the police investigation got no further than my neighbour.

The District Engineer was also in great demand by the military in that important defence area. They asked for cavities to be made in the brickwork of railway bridges in the Harwich area so that, if necessary, explosives could be placed in them and the bridges blown up if the enemy invaded our shores. Later on, they wanted the cavities opened up, live explosives put in and the top bricks replaced. Then along came a new Division with other ideas and the explosives had to be taken out again.

We were fortunate in the Ipswich district that air raids did comparatively little damage to railway property. A bomb fell between the rails on the Harwich branch line near Manningtree station. It only appeared to have made a deep hole of small circumference which was soon filled in. Early one morning, soon afterwards, the astute driver of a light engine spotted a gaping hole four feet ahead of him. He was able to stop the engine before reaching the hole and to warn the signalman.

The crater was found to be at the same spot where the bomb had dropped, and it was soon realised it was, in fact, the same bomb. It had exploded at the bottom of the shaft which the Engineer's gang had filled up. C.B. Smith likened the damage to a huge wine decanter, his men had filled in the neck but not the huge empty bowl the bomb had made when it exploded. This had collapsed, leaving the crater. It was provident the light engine was the first to travel along the Harwich branch that morning.

I shall never forget the air raid on Halesworth early in 1940. At 2.00pm on Saturday, C.B. called at my house and we went off in my car to Halesworth. We drove through a snowstorm to find there had been a direct hit on the Station Master's house, and Herbert Holland, the Station Master, his wife and a young girl who was helping in the house, had been killed outright. I was told by a member of the Observer Corps that a German reconnaissance plane had been coming over the town round about noon, on the same course and at the same height, on several Saturdays and light Ack. Ack. batteries had been sited around the town as a reception party for its next visit. When the plane arrived, as anticipated, it banked just beyond the town as usual and the guns on the higher positions opened up. The plane appeared to be hit and dived right down on the town and at a very low level, pulled out and released a number of small bombs in the railway station area. One of them killed Herbert Holland and the other unfortunate people who were sheltering in a cupboard. The plane was hit by a battery at Holton and went down in the sea off Southwold.

It was no joyride driving a car at night in wartime. Headlamps had to be fitted with black tin masks, with narrow slits in front through which weak shafts of light were projected onto the road. Drivers could only see for a short distance ahead. Side lamps were rendered ineffective by an Order that two thicknesses of tissue paper had to be placed at the back of each glass.

My journey back to Ipswich in the dark and in a raging blizzard was a nightmare drive. There was a thick layer of snow on the ground which was gradually getting thicker as we made our way slowly to the main Great Yarmouth to Ipswich road. Here there were no hedges to help us keep on the road. The road and the fields on either side merged themselves into one expansive white field; the swirling snow froze on the windscreen and found its way into the narrow slits in the mask, literally blindfolding the car. I had to periodically brave the fierce elements to clear out the slits so we could see to proceed on our way. I saw only one other car during the whole journey and that had been abandoned at the side of the road. It took three times as long to get home as it did to get to Halesworth. Irene was thankful when I arrived home and so was I.

My guardian angel looked after me one winter's afternoon when we were returning home from one of our rare visits to Cambridge. I had forgotten to remove the radiator muff and when we were about two miles out of the town the windscreen was bespattered with a brownish liquid and the car stopped. The water in the radiator had boiled over, the water hose had burst and everything under the bonnet was smothered with a glutinous mixture of water and antifreeze.

The light was fading, and the situation seem hopeless. My first impulse was to fill the radiator and I walked across the road to a roadhouse a little way off to ask for a can of water. There were several men sitting at tables drinking tea and as I passed them, looking straight ahead at the proprietor, something extraordinary happened, I heard a voice call out "What are you doing here Mr Cobb?" I was almost overcome with amazement and relief when I saw that the owner of the voice was an experienced motor car engineer who, believe it or not, used to service my old Clyno when we were both very much younger, in Norwich. I had lost sight of him for years, and he was now in charge of the railway road motor department in Cambridge. He had just dropped into the roadhouse with his two mechanics, on their way back to his depot. C.B. Smith was surprised when he saw me emerge from the house with three men and a can of water. They brought their tools over and after they had spent about twenty minutes cleaning and repairing; the car started up and we were on our way again. It seemed a miracle I should meet him at a time of need.

On several occasions we visited the site of the fifteen inch rail-mounted gun on the Ipswich to Felixstowe line near Orwell. It was on a spur built by our Engineer's department staff. It had a sliding top like the roof of a large hut, this obscured the gun from enemy observation, and was drawn back when the gun was in action.

C.B. was invited to watch the gun being fired for the first time. I was in the road talking to the village constable when it went off without warning. There was a mighty 'boo—oom' which nearly made us jump out of our skins; a nearby house had all the windows broken and it was rumoured that the live shell missed the target out at sea by nearly three quarters of a mile.

Life was never dull. The Felix Hotel at Felixstowe, one of finest of the LNER hotels, came under the District Engineer, Ipswich, for maintenance and C.B. was often called in by the Resident Manager when some special work was required to be done. This generally involved the two of us having a splendid lunch and a game of snooker to while away the lunch time, before the serious work was commenced.

There was one occasion when we went down in the afternoon and we took his daughter, Monica, with us. She and I were sitting in the lounge looking out to sea, while C.B. was somewhere in the hotel with the Resident Manager. We saw a small naval vessel ploughing a straight course parallel with the beach, and when it was in line with us the bow suddenly sank, the rest of the boat tilted upwards and disappeared under the sea in a matter of seconds. We saw none of the crew at any time, and we heard no sound of an explosion (perhaps it was because we were too far away). The boat went down so gently there was little or no displacement of water or any sign of floating objects. All we could see from our window high above the cliff top was a wide expanse of sea with not a single ship anywhere. It all seemed so unreal and we just sat and stared at each other in amazement. The

177

incident was never made public and I'm still wondering what really happened.

I had been with the District Engineer for nearly two years when I was recalled to take over the duties of a Class 4 Goods canvasser who had been given two choices. He could either join the Forces at the next "call up" or apply for a Station Master's position which would exempt him from Military Service. He chose the latter course and he was appointed Station Master at Westerfield.

I was glad to have a permanent job again, but would miss the generous car allowance I had been getting which exceeded the price I paid for the car, besides which a motor mechanic had come over from Norwich once a month to service the DG & PM's private car and mine, and spares, repairs and petrol had been provided free. It looked as though my bonanza was over, but my good luck stuck to me. The railway owned car which went with the job was loaned to the District Engineer and I was given permission to use my own car, mileage allowance boosting my earning to those of much higher graded clerks who had to sit at their desks all day.

The word "canvassing" was a misnomer because at that time the Railways were employed to the limit of their capacities moving war supplies and vast tonnages of hard core and other materials for the chain of aerodromes then under construction in East Anglia.

Sleepy country stations mushroomed within enlarged sidings and yards where upwards of forty trucks a day were dealt with. Large numbers had to be held back en route until destination stations were in a position to handle them.

Two years later, in 1943, an unfortunate illness was responsible for the premature retirement of Joe Nickalls, our Chief Canvasser, and the stagnation barrier was, at long last, broken. I was promoted to Ipswich canvasser, Class 3 and I was thankful my long spell in grade 4 was over, but not so happy with the prospect of gaining three shillings and ten pence a week with the first two years and losing thirty shillings or more car allowance as the duties of the Ipswich canvasser could be done on foot.

Once again, I was lucky. My District Officer liked the look of my private car better than the railway-owned car the company provided him with, so he arranged for his to be sent out of the Ipswich district and hired mine. Thus, I continued to receive a car allowance and had the use of my car at week-ends.

When I arrived in Ipswich to take up my appointment in 1937, there was a huge board outside the station welcoming visitors to the town and proclaiming a population of 90,000 inhabitants. I thought I had come to a less important place then Norwich which had a population of 126,000 but I soon found it was more important industrially and rail freight tonnages and receipts exceeded those at Norwich.

When I started my new job, it was a revelation to discover the extent and importance of the large and expanding firms in Ipswich. There was Reavell's near the station, making air and gas compressors, pneumatic tools and vacuum pumps, WA & AC Churchman Ltd. who are associated with the Imperial Tobacco Company, on the top of whose works I used to stand on Sunday mornings, exchanging semaphore messages by lamp and flags, with other Home Guard signallers who were in a church tower on the other side of town. Clothing factories were making suits, overcoats, corsets and ladies' under-garments. Ransomes Sims & Jefferies Ltd. employed over 3,000 men, producing lawn mowers, electric road vehicles and trolley buses. Ransomes & Rapier specialised in railway turntables, hoists, cranes and large overseas projects like sluice gates. ER & F Turner made flour milling plant for all parts of the world, and Crane Bennett Ltd., associated with a Crane Company of the USA, produced, among other articles, equipment for water heating installations.

The Head Office of Fisons, the fertiliser producers, was then in Ipswich and the firm was absorbing kindred small firms so rapidly that their Transport Manager, Mr Watling, had not been advised a particular firm had been taken over, when I presented him with an account for settlement which the newly acquired firm had endorsed "Refer to Fisons for payment". There were Docks covering an area of 26 acres, flour mills, breweries, yeast makers, a bacon factory and other industries and trades of international repute. The geographical position of the town, 69½ miles from London, made it an ideal centre, and important firms like English Electric Co. and Callenders Cables established offices to develop their business in East Anglia and beyond.

It was a very interesting and satisfying job, but Irene and I yearned to return to our native city, Norwich, which to us was 'the Mecca of the East.' We were constantly zipping over at weekends, seeing our parents and friends, and I rarely missed a Norwich City football match at Carrow Road on Saturday afternoons. I had never given up hope of getting back to my old office in Norwich and continued to attend Masonic Lodges and my Lodge of Instruction every Friday evening in the winter months, returning home from Norwich by the 11.25pm train. It was a tiring journey with a wait of an hour at Haughley and I would arrive home about 2 o'clock in the morning. When the lights were dimmed in the train it was a sign there were enemy bombers overhead and it was then I was concerned about Irene, wondering if she had to get out of bed and carry our baby down the garden, and into the dugout, no mean feat in the blackout. I was particularly worried the night I was the only civilian in a stuffy and dimly lighted compartment packed tightly with soldiers returning to their units. I fell asleep during the long wait at Haughley and woke up with the train stopped at a station. To my dismay it was Colchester, 20 miles beyond Ipswich. It was past 2 o'clock in the morning and the next train to Ipswich was at 6.30am which would get me home at break-fast time.

Irene would be frantic with worry, especially as the German bombers had been over in the night. Once again, my good fortune prevailed. The night clerk had a record of a trainload of army tanks passing through Colchester during the previous day, and the light engine would be returning non-stop to Ipswich at 3.30am He telephoned to Control asking if the engine driver could be asked to stop at Colchester to pick up a railway official. To my great relief the driver stopped. I had turned my light overcoat inside out to keep it clean and I stood unobtrusively on the footplate, watching the fireman as he expertly clicked the underside of his shovel on the bottom edge of the fire box while he constantly threw coal into the blazing hole. I arrived home about 5 o'clock in the morning and quietly slipped into bed without waking Irene. The Lord be praised, she had not missed me.

After the VE Day celebrations, my thoughts went back to my passenger canvassing job which was discontinued when war broke out. I was now in a higher grade, but I was anxious the great potential in party travel would be exploited again when the railways got back to normal, so I prepared a comprehensive report giving a complete picture of canvassing prospects in the Ipswich district. My District Officer told me it was "The answer to a maiden's prayer" as it coincided with a request from the Passenger Manager at Liverpool Street for his views on the future prospects of passenger canvassing.

It was a fortunate piece of opportunism which brought to notice my enthusiasm and preference for passenger work, and it may have triggered off my rapid promotion from Ipswich canvasser Class 3 to Head of Development, Special Class, within the space of three years which was not bad going for a chap who had stagnated Class 4 for twenty-five years.

Chapter 17
LNER — Back To Norwich

Soon after the end of the war, arrangements were made to re-organise goods and passenger canvassing throughout the railways and the positions of Head of Development, Special Class and Deputy Head of Development, Class I were advertised. I was disappointed the Deputy Head would be graded Class 1 which seemed to me to put me out of the running, a 3rd Class canvasser like me having no chance against the rush of applications that would be made by Class 2 clerical staff from all over the railway system. Bertie Withers, chief of the Passenger Section at Ipswich, went to Norwich for an interview for the Deputy Head position with a second batch of candidates, and came back to Ipswich feeling despondent because he had been unable to answer questions put to him which were, he considered, irrelevant to the job.

DISTRICT GOODS & PASSENGER MANAGER,
L.N.E.R.
IPSWICH.

RW/PM

18th.July,1946.
S.VL.8/441.

MEMO TO MR.F.G.G.COBB,
IPSWICH D.G.&.P.M.O.

VACANCY LIST NO.8. VACANCY NO.441.
CLASS 1 CLERK. NORWICH D.G.&.P.M.O.

I am pleased to inform you that it has been agreed to your appointment to the above position at a commencing salary of £335 per annum.

I am informing the Norwich D.G.&.P.M. that the date of transfer will be 5th.August.

Some weeks later, when it seemed almost certain that the lucky man had been selected, my District Officer asked me why I had not put in for the Norwich vacancy. I respectfully informed him it would have meant jumping a grade and I did not believe in miracles. "Put in for it" he said in a casual sort of way. I did just that and in July 1946 was called to Norwich for an interview and got the job.

Irene and I were in the seventh heaven of delight, we sold our house in Ipswich and within weeks we had moved to St. Williams Way, Thorpe St. Andrew in Norwich.

It was wonderful to be back with my old colleagues after an absence of a ten years and an exciting future lay ahead for us.

My first sustained efforts at canvassing were at Lowestoft which I visited by car every day. I opened an office on the Herring Market to maintain contact with fish merchants during the 1946 East Anglian herring fishing season. This extended from the beginning of October to the second or third week in December.

I was like an innocent abroad but soon found out that a trawler landed fish of the demersal group such as cod, plaice, haddock, skate, dogfish, all classed as 'white fish', and drifters landed fish of the pelagic type such as herring, mackerel and sprats, so that when a merchant asked me if I would like some white fish I knew I would be taking home some prime plaice in a rush mat.

Herring fishing commenced in Scotland in June and Scottish drifters followed the fish down the east coast, until they reached Great Yarmouth and Lowestoft in early October, where they augmented the local fleets. The highest number of vessels fishing from the two ports was 1,163 in the 1913 season, when about 87% of the catch was cured or pickled and exported to Germany and Russia; a trade which ceased after the First World War. I can remember, in 1913, seeing huge stacks of barrels standing on the quay at Great Yarmouth awaiting export, and also all the Scottish fisher girls who flocked to the two ports in their thousands to dexterously gut the herrings. They lived in the front rooms of terraced houses which had been stripped of carpets and furniture because of the extreme pungency of their clothing. I have no record of the number of special trains that conveyed them from Scotland and back again, but in 1929 fourteen were laid on for between 6,000 and 7,000 lassies. By 1946 numbers had diminished to between 1,500 and 2,000.

It was a new experience for me visiting the fish merchants at their offices on the herring market. They were completely different to the men of commerce I had been used to meeting — friendly and generous, but a community apart, living in close proximity, selling the same commodity and jealously keeping their business to themselves. Some even put plain labels to cover the address labels which were fixed to their boxes of fish waiting to be collected by private hauliers from outside their offices on the fish wharf and carted to the fish sidings at Lowestoft Central station. The plain labels were to conceal the names and addresses of their customers from fellow merchants.

My District Officer and myself entertained a number of the principal merchants at a luncheon at a local hotel at the end of each season, and the repast was followed by a meeting reviewing past season's transport arrangements. It was enjoyed and appreciated by the industry and helped to ensure the smooth working of rail traffic in the season that followed.

There were 123 drifters operating at Lowestoft in the 1946 season and 132,894 crans, valued at £510,140 were landed. The major proportion of the herrings were allocated by the Ministry of Food to the home trade and a good percentage were dispatched by rail by special trains run daily during the season to Western, Midland and Northern areas, to the Southern Region and to North Eastern and Scottish ports. Fish was also dispatched to London each evening by the regular goods train services although road transport had already commenced to make inroads into that hitherto secure rail traffic. That traffic practically fell into the laps of road competitors when the Ministry of Food, who controlled the price of herring and paid carriage charges on the fish whether it was dispatched by rail or road, made a condition that the charges were inclusive of picking up at the fish wharf and delivery at the destination. If the fish was dispatched by rail it involved the merchant in a charge of 2/6d. per cran (28 stones) for the cartage of his fish from the wharf to Lowestoft Central station which he would have to pay himself. It is obvious he would choose road transport if a service was available.

The Transport Act of 1947 passed by the Labour Government gave the 'coup de grâce' to rail traffic at Lowestoft. The railways, road haulage and other undertakings were nationalised and vested to the British Transport Commission. The Road Haulage Association and the Railways were integrated, the rail District Manager at Norwich was made responsible for quoting rates for both rail and road transport and it did not matter whether the fish was handled by rail or road so long as the revenue went into the coffers of the British Transport Commission.

I read recently the last consignment of by-product from the Lowestoft fish market was dispatched by rail on September 27th 1973 thus breaking the link between rail and the fishing industry that had lasted for 100 years.

It is the appropriate time to recall the considerable contributions railways made to the prosperity of the fishing industry and to Lowestoft itself, not only in providing the harbour facilities at the railway owned docks, passenger services for visitors, fish and fish workers, and freight train services for large tonnages of ancillary traffics important to the industry, like coal for bunkering the drifters and the trawlers which were still mainly steam propelled. In 1946, 91,000 tonnes were received at Lowestoft. Salt, too, was brought in by rail from the English salt mines to the tune of 1,600 tonnes in 1918. Later it was only 502 tonnes in 1946 because the English mines were unable to maintain supplies and therefore they had to be augmented by imports from Sardinia and Spain.

Chapter 18 — LNER To Retirement

The integration of rail and road brought about by nationalisation created a situation where two District Managers, one rail and the other road transport, travelled together to Gaymer's Cider Works, at Attleborough, and persuaded the Managing Director to transfer regular consignments of cider being dispatched to customers in the East and West Ridings of Yorkshire, from rail to road and the firm's own vehicle to Road Haulage Association vehicles. Road transport gave a quicker transit and the move was advantageous to the British Transport Commission, but it found no favour in me as I realised it had enabled road transport to gain a foothold in the firm. Ever since my first visit to their premises in 1930, when Mr W.C.C. Gaymer proudly informed me rail was being used exclusively, I had looked upon Wm. Gaymer & Son Ltd. as the sacred cow of the railway and on my frequent visits I had tried hard to keep things that way, and now road transport had sadly gained a foothold.

The Transport Act of 1953 stimulated road competition throughout the country. The Road Haulage Association was denationalised, and a Disposal Board set up which offered the whole of the Association's fleet of 29,300 vehicles for sale. The BRS Depot at Harling Road had provided the vehicles for the cider traffic to the Ridings of Yorkshire and those vehicles were bought from the Disposal Board by the Depot Manager. Very soon he had entered into an arrangement with Gaymers and the railway era had come to an end.

If, prior to denationalisation of road haulage, I had tried to delude myself the wind of change had not arrived when I was about my canvassing duties, it must have whistled round my ears the morning in 1947 when I called on a Managing Director of tremendous drive and charm who was building up a business in frozen fruit which extended to nationwide importance and a great future for himself. I was armed with specially reduced rail rates for regular consignments of frozen fruit to Grimsby in refrigerated rail containers. He informed me our rates were still too high and was kind enough to tell me the reason why. A fairly elderly man, wearing a cap and leaning on a walking stick came to see him one morning. He was busy and felt half inclined to pass the man on to his Manager but listened to what he had to say. He wanted to convey the firm's output of frozen foods to Grimsby by his own road vehicles. He was prepared to build a six ton refrigerated container fitted on a trailer which would be hauled by a six ton refrigerated motor lorry and the combined load of twelve tons per unit would permit him to quote a low rate. He was passed on to the firm's Engineer, specifications were drawn up, the vehicles were built, and the man got the business, which was soon extended to embrace the transport of frozen products from a large concern at Great Yarmouth.

"You cannot compete against that" said the Managing Director commiserating with me. It was all too true, and it made the work of a goods canvasser frustrating and unrewarding.

Where there were regular flows of traffic, efforts were made to induce senders to use rail containers but it became evident road operators could move heavy tonnages from door to door at rates the railways could not compete against, and we found ourselves being offered container loads of articles of little weight, like baking tins, a container load around two tons, which road operators would not handle because the pay-load was unprofitable.

My finest and perhaps busiest year was 1949 when I achieved two ambitions. I was made Head of Development, Norwich district, and on the social side was installed as Worshipful Master of one of the largest Masonic lodges in Norfolk which made all my war-time night travelling between Ipswich and Norwich well worthwhile and it also involved, apart from my own Lodge duties, visiting lodges in Norwich and Norfolk as one of the travelling circus of reigning Masters.

My duties as Head of Development were far from frustrating. It seems strange that railway officials with access to cars rarely found train services suited their convenience. I was no exception, visiting principal traders at regular intervals, travelling with one or other of the eight canvassers under my control, one of whom was the canvasser whom the panel of Headquarters people preferred to me way back in 1935 when I presented myself wearing spats. He had stagnated whilst I had gained in experience and authority. We were good friends. I attended local markets and the Corn Exchanges at Norwich and Kings Lynn and found time to perform office duties.

On the passenger side, liaison was maintained with our Associated Bus Company in respect to applications to the Traffic Commissioners by private operators for licences to run Excursions and Tours and Stage Coach services and I opposed many such applications at Traffic Court hearings in Cambridge.

Frequent meetings had to be attended at Liverpool Street station which were spiced by splendid luncheons and such regalings were the high spots of regular meetings at Norwich Thorpe station with representatives of travel agents, Cooks, Pickfords, Wortley, Polytours and Sterling.

There were conducted tours of London and Cambridge for outdoor representatives in order to enable them to get first-hand knowledge of what they could offer to party organisers. I also decided to accompany them and in the reverse direction I arranged for similar conducted tours to Norwich and the Norfolk Broads for outdoor representatives in other districts.

Broads Tours, Wroxham readily placed a boat at our disposal and now I was able to prevail upon the late R.H. Mottram, a great author and authority on Norwich (and the first soldier to greet me at the Norwich Drill Hall when I joined up in 1914), to act as guide. The tours bore fruit in abundance and as a direct result of the outdoor representatives' enthusiasm for what they had seen, many trainloads of 550 and more schoolchildren came to Norwich and the Broads on day trips and are still coming.

We arranged lots of special train for parties from Norwich to London and Windsor. There were trips on the Thames, to Tom Arnold's ice shows at Wembley and the Royal Tournament at Earls Court. Irene and I went on several occasions on these excursions at the invitation of the organisers.

We owned a Bell & Howell 16mm sound projector and plenty of feature films which we showed to Women's Institutes and at other meetings in Norfolk. They were in the afternoons and evenings and myself and another operator would happily sing 'Jerusalem' and often judge the WI ladies' competitions. On two occasions the District Operating Superintendent asked me to pour oil on troubled waters in his department. A garrulous and influential squire had sworn at a porter at a country station. That might have been accepted as the squire's privilege before the Second World War, but the porter had been emancipated and threatened to report the incident to his union. The Station Master had referred the matter to his superior in Norwich and it was left to me. I knew of the squire's reputation for being outspoken and remembered a Court case where he had appeared because he had taken a stick to a boy he had caught in his orchard. I made an appointment to see him and drove down a lane bearing no indication to where it might lead. I stopped a woman coming in the opposite direction and she told me that it was the drive to his mansion but, said the woman, "Drive slowly for if the squire sees you going fast, he will order you off his estate". I drove slowly to the house and his charming wife showed me into his presence in the library and he immediately took the wind out of my sails by telling me he had been wrong and offered to apologise to the porter. I went to the station and resolved the matter peacefully and finally.

The other occasion was just the reverse, a porter at a small country station had sworn at a retired major who was of such great importance in the county that he wrote a personal letter of complaint to Lord Hurcombe, Chairman of the British Transport Commission which started off with "Dear Hurcombe" and asked for the porter to be put in his place. My instructions were clear. I had to see the Major and placate him so that he did not bother Lord Hurcombe again. I saw the porter first, but he was not helpful. He was "not going to stand for anybody, no matter who he was, coming to the station and riding the high horse with him." Then I went up to see the Major who discussed the matter in a reasonable way and agreed to talk to the porter. I took the porter along and was relieved when the two settled their differences amicably and shook hands. I went back to Norwich highly delighted with my morning's work.

I retired from the railway in 1961 and can honestly say there was no other job I'd rather have done even though the authorities were, at that time, parsimonious with their salaries and expenses. I had a very full life at work, at play and in a loving household, so much so that I rarely, if ever, gave a thought to my soldiering days until the memories were rekindled by the reappearance of the sketch and my visit to France in 1974.

Fifty Years With Railways

AFTER 50 years' service with the railways, Mr. Fred Cobb, of 29, St. William's Way, Norwich, retired on June 17th.

At Thorpe Station yesterday, he was presented with a farewell gift of two garden chairs from his colleagues. The presentation was made by Mr. G. W. Brimyard, district commercial officer.

Mr. Cobb began his railway career in 1911 when, at the age of 14, he joined the clerical staff at Victoria Station, Norwich.

In 1912 he moved to Thorpe, where he remained until May, 1914, when he enlisted in the Norfolk Regiment. He served in France and Italy, and was mentioned in dispatches.

After the war, he returned to Thorpe Station, and worked there up to 1937, when he was transferred to Ipswich. In 1946, he came back to Norwich, as deputy head of the development section.

In 1949 he became head of this section, and when reorganisation was carried out in January, 1958, he was appointed head of the development rates and fares section.

Gardening has always been one of Mr. Cobb's chief interests.

Mr. Fred Cobb (right) and Mr. G. W. Brimyard (District Commercial Officer, British Railways) trying the two garden chairs which were presented to Mr. Cobb to mark his retirement.

Eastern Evening News — June 21st 1961

Courtesy of the Archant Library

191

Chapter 19 — Sentimental Journey
My Pilgrimage to France

It was only a matter of weeks after finding the sketch which is the preface of this book that I find myself alone on the 6.40am train at Norwich Thorpe station at the start of my visit to Hinges, which I last saw in 1918.

I had the sketch with me and in the seclusion of a first-class compartment my thoughts wandered to the paths along which my army boots had often trod and to the lake in which countless toads sat motionless with their heads just out of the water. Their ceaseless croaking and the sound of firing of machine guns, trench mortars and heavy guns from the distant battle area, kept me awake the first few nights I was at the château but I soon got used to it, as I had done the year before, with the constant roar of the sea pounding on the shore, when I was in my comfortable billet at Lowestoft.

A stately round brick tower built on top of a huge mass of rock stood in a setting of tall trees and reminded me of scenery in Scotland, instilling in me a feeling of nostalgia. From the pinnacle of the tower, a thin iron mast decorated with scrollwork rose high in the sky. A path alongside the lake passed through a grotto in the rock to gardens beyond. In the distance, beyond flat hedgeless fields, the church and tall belfry in the Grand Place in Bethune, five miles distant, could clearly be seen. To the left, a long line of barrage balloons signalled the proximity of the front line. At night, very lights, beautiful in their colour, gave a continuous firework display like the end of summer season carnival at Great Yarmouth.

It was wonderfully challenging and relaxing in the grotto. The quiet scene made a profound impression on my young mind when I found myself alone for the first time in the veritable Aladdin's Cave and I stood in silent awe and amazement as the light seeped in through two opposite openings and revealed rock formations like huge stalactites which were mirrored in placid water inside the grotto.

It seemed so unreal in that war-torn land. In a few short hours I will see what difference two world wars and half a century of time had made.

I thought of the last time I had made the journey on the 10.35pm mail train from Norwich Thorpe to Liverpool Street after ten days unforgettable leave in 1917. It was the train on which the majority of soldiers returned to their Units after leave of absence. I shall never forget the animated and emotional scenes on the dimly lighted platform as wives and sweethearts said goodbye to their loved one and many a lass saw her khaki-clad lover for the last time when he boarded that "heartbreak" train. My compartment was full of soldiers with their rifles and kitbags and as the train steamed into the blackness of the night there was a deathly silence as each soldier, feeling the last burning kisses, sat choking back his emotions. I was no less affected and a snatch of a poem I learnt at school came back to me-

"There were sudden partings,
Such as press the life from out young hearts,
And choking sighs which ne'er might be repeated,
Who would guess if evermore should meet those mutual eyes,
Since upon night so sweet,
Such awful morn could rise."*

It was all so different this time, and I settled down with notebook and pen to pass the time away recording my experiences, having not the slightest notion it would develop into this autobiography of an ordinary railwayman of the old school.

By way of contrast with my army days, I travelled on the Golden Arrow from Victoria station and sat in the first-class

---

*Extract from *The Eve of Waterloo* by Lord Byron

lounge of the cross-channel steamer, 'Invicta' instead of in the hold of a troopship with hundreds of other soldiers.

I booked in at an hotel in Bethune and, my first thoughts being of Irene, I went into a stationer's shop for a postcard and a stamp. I asked the lady behind the counter the best way to get to Hinges and when I told her the reason for my intended visit it brought two elderly ladies on the scene. They were living in Bethune in 1914/18 and I was thrilled with my first conversation in France as it was the most unusual thing to happen to me at my time of life. I walked to the Grand Place and gazed at the same tall belfry I had seen from the Château's grounds at Hinges. The square had been transformed from the drabness of war, when there was hardly a young man or woman to be seen, to a modern shopping centre buzzing with smartly dressed citizens and there was still a small baker's shop tucked away in a corner. I went in and bought two sticky cakes as an excuse to see inside. It could very well have been the same shop but the man who served me had not been in it for long enough to remember the baker or his youngest daughter who married little Sergeant Parrott.

I was the only passenger on an old service bus which left Bethune at 7.55am the next morning, and as we drove along the country road towards Hinges my hair tingled with excitement as I saw the same flat hedgeless fields on either side. I was back in the past and gasped with surprise when I recognised a brick shrine on the side of the road where the natives in 1916 and 1917 reverently crossed themselves as they passed and repassed on their way to and from Bethune. Then the altar was bright with fresh flowers provided by the nuns from the nearby convent and the figure of the Virgin Mary was a symbol of hope in those dark days of war. Now that shrine is but a brick shed weathered with the years, its rusty iron door is chained and padlocked and a peep through a grill in the door revealed an interior long since abandoned. I was glad it was still there to rekindle my memory of its former saintly dignity.

I stepped off the bus into a street deserted, except for a woman standing at the door of her cottage evidently curious to see who the bus had brought in. When I looked in her direction, she shot off indoors leaving the door open for further spying if I moved away. There was nobody else I could see to talk to, so I walked over to her open door and she cautiously advanced. I showed her my sketch and she told me the Château was not there now, but the tower was in the garden of Monsieur Le Maire who would let me inspect it if I went along and asked him.

He looked surprised when I walked up to him in his vegetable garden and told him my mission. The Château had been destroyed by German shell fire. His house had been built in the grounds of the Château, the lake had been filled in and was now his vegetable garden. I could see the tower and the entrance to the grotto. The tower looked the same as it did fifty years before, but the grotto had deteriorated into a store for the Maire's fruit trays. There was no lake to mirror the light from the opening in the rock formation, the only thing left was the tranquillity and as I stood and stared for a few minutes I had a feeling my mind's picture had been badly smudged by the passage of time, but felt grateful I had survived the long years to see the original again.

HINGES – Ruins of the Chateau

The Germans shelled the village and, within minutes, all the inhabitants became refugees.

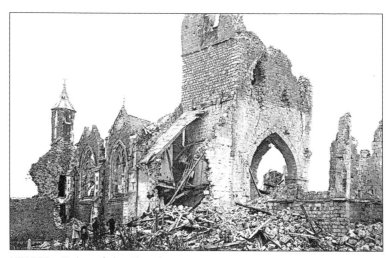

HINGES – Ruins of the Church

"How small the world seems to be now", I thought later when the Maire told me his son was working in Skegness.

It was barely 9.00am when I went off to the tiny village street to look for the cottage where Madame had served meals so quietly and efficiently. When I passed by, the inquisitive woman was still at her 'look out' position.

I must have looked like an Englishman with my dark suit and with a camera slung over my shoulder. I walked down the deserted street, and even the dogs seem to sense from the sound of my footsteps there was a stranger about, although they could not see me. They all started barking in the distance. There were no cottages where I thought they used to be and, as I stood contemplating my next move an old lady of about 80 years of age, toothless and tiny, walked from her bungalow to her garden gate and stayed there. I begged her pardon for my intrusion, told her, in my own interpretation of the French language, I was a one-time British soldier stationed at the Château in 1916, and was looking for a cottage where a lady cooked our meals.

She hailed a lady friend who was passing on her bicycle (she looked like a district nurse) saying "He's asking about Marie". In actual fact it was Marie's mother I had asked about, but I realised she had possibly been dead some years. The two French ladies decided I must talk to a Monsieur (the name never registered with me), and I followed the woman with the bicycle to the house next door. She walked straight in the front door with me just behind her, to be met by a small man about my own age, neatly dressed and wearing a black beret. He looked surprised at the sudden intrusion, and his daughter came to see what was going on. After introducing me the woman left, and I was asked into the living room where I was treated like one of the family. The man took me into the drawing-room and showed me an enlarged frame photograph of Marie, who had been his wife and who died at the age of 66 years. Then the three of us sat looking at photographs and picture postcards of the damage done to the church, the Château and its environment by the German bombardment on that fateful day in 1918 when the whole village had to be evacuated within minutes. One of the postcards was of the Château with its facade still recognisable though badly damaged beyond repair. The dormer windows of the attic were there too, reminding me where I used to sleep and from where I made my sketch. It made my day when he gave me that postcard and two others. He took me into his garden and showed me the remains of the foundations of the cottages and then I took my leave of the two most friendly French people who gave me a strong invitation to call on them the next time I was in Hinges.

They were disappointed when I told them I would not be coming again but I knew I could never recapture the thrills which I had already experienced in such a short time. I went into the village café, eager to have a longer look at postcards of the Château and the church, over a cup of coffee. I was soon telling the two ladies running the cafe of my good luck in meeting their neighbours and the elder said her mother would love to talk to me as she had often told her of the British soldiers who were in the Château in its grounds in the 1914/18 war. With my consent she fetched a neatly dressed lady of 72 from the rear of the shop, she confirmed what her daughter had said. It amazed me when she went on to say she remembered us moving off to Italy in November

1917 and returning to Hinges three months later. I had truly forgotten about that move until she reminded me of it. The two younger ladies listened with great interest to our conversation and were also intrigued with my sketch as it was the first picture they had seen of the lake and garden which had been devastated by the Germans before they were born.

My coffee was cold, and I decided not to wear out my welcome so off I went to the end of the village street, a very short distance indeed. There was no sign of life at the bungalow of the old lady I had spoken to about Madame but on my return, she walked down to her garden gate as she had done before and beckoned me over. "I want to show you something Monsieur." she said to me. I followed her to her door and stood on the threshold. "*Venez*" she requested, and I entered the spic-and-span living room-cum-kitchen. She pointed to an enlarged framed photograph of a good-looking French Officer, which was hanging on the wall. "That is my son" she proudly exclaimed "He is 54 years of age and his father was a British soldier who he has never seen". She talked rapidly and mostly in patois but I understood the purpose of her long story which I listened to patiently and sympathetically. I realised that when I first spoke to her and she found out I was a *soldat britannique* who was with the XI Corps it had unlocked sad memories of the past, when the soldier who had courted her in 1917, left Hinges and never answered her appealing letters. All her efforts to trace him had failed and she was left to bring her son up on her own.

We used to sing a song which went *Après la guerre finie, soldat Anglais parti, Mademoiselle beaucoup fâchée, avec une petite bébé.* I had now come face to face with the tragic reality of that parody and felt sorry for the brave little woman whose life had been brightened by the devotion of her son who had provided her with the nice bungalow and saw that she wants for nothing in her old age. I wonder what the father's feelings would have been if he had stood in my place and had seen that photograph of the French officer hanging in its place of honour.

The thrills I had unexpectedly enjoyed in the few hours I had been in Hinges mixed with compassion as I walked from

198

the cosy bungalow. There was nothing more I could do or see in the tiny village and I started to walk the five miles to Bethune which I had done so many times in my early twenties. It was not so easy at 70 years plus and I was glad to stop at a village about half-way to enquire if I could get a lift for the rest of the journey, but my efforts proved futile. The man I spoke to called his wife and son from their house and they joined in the conversation afterwards inviting me inside for a beer. I felt at home with all the French people I had spoken to and their friendliness made my long trip completely worthwhile, and something to remember with pleasure for the rest of my days.

I was tired but contented when I sat down to a celebration meal at the hotel and, after another look round Bethune, settled in early in preparation for the sightseeing tour of Lille and Arras I had planned for the next day. I shall never know what irresistible force made me decide, when I lay in bed that night, that I must go home to Irene. I was just as determined the next morning, so I checked out of the hotel and took the train to Calais instead of to Lille. I was disappointed Irene was not at home when I arrived the same evening. The curtains had not been drawn although it was quite dark. The postcard which I had sent from Bethune was propped up on the mantelpiece. It told her I would be home on the Friday evening, and now I had turned up a day too soon. I appeased my hunger after the long journey and set off in my car to find her. I met the train which she usually arrived on when she went to see our daughter Janette and her family, but eventually found her at the house of one of her sisters. The sister's husband had died suddenly and unexpectedly the night I made up my mind to come home. Irene was helping her sister in her bereavement and was surprised and relieved to see me.

Was it a coincidence or a premonition that decided me to cut short my planned holiday? I am convinced it was the same invisible power that took me from the dangers of the trenches to Hinges, that has guided my path through life and now brought me back to my devoted partner when she needed me most. It was the Almighty.

Still Going Strong In 1973

Appendix

A Selection of Articles Written for *The London & North Eastern Railway Magazine*

		Page
July 1929	The LNER in Norwich	202
January 1931	The Canning Industry in Lowestoft	204
April 1932	Quaint Buildings and Streets of Norwich	206
September 1932	Cromer and the Crab Fishing Industry	208
December 1932	"Fishergate, Norwich"	210
March 1933	The Romance of Norfolk Cyder Making	211
April 1934	A Peep at Carrow Works	213
April 1936	The Norwich Rose Industry	218
July 1937	The Norfolk Broadland	221

The L.N.E.R. in Norwich.

By H. C. R. CALVER, Stationmaster.

NORWICH lies serenely tucked away in a corner of Norfolk, far away from the trunk line on which the Newcastle non-stop express thunders its way northwards, and is partly surrounded by the Broads, those fascinating and alluring stretches of water. So easy of access is it to the many seaside resorts of the Norfolk coast that the importance of the city itself, either from a railway, commercial or historical point of view, is overshadowed by its beautiful surroundings.

The city is built on low-lying ground, and one realises this when viewing it from Mousehold Heath, the high parts of which are reputed to be on a level with the cathedral spire.

The River Wensum wends its way placidly through the city, and can be seen at various parts both as commercial factor and as a pleasure resort.

This article is more concerned with the L.N.E.R. activities in the city and its importance as a feeding point to the numerous single-line branches in East Anglia.

The present passenger station was built in 1886, and is a handsome structure of red brick, with bath stone facings surmounted by a dome. It has a large circulating area for vehicular traffic. There are five platforms and one middle road, and each platform is fitted with exit gates which lead to a concourse and the various station offices. Quick platform clearance is attained, as all exit gates can be open at the same time.

To all intents Norwich is a terminus, but through express trains London to Cromer or Yarmouth are diverted at Swing Bridge Junction via Wensum Curve, thus avoiding the city. All trains arriving at Norwich are re-engined before proceeding via Thorpe Junction to the coast or Londonwards.

With the exception of the down goods reception road, the whole of the traffic for Thorpe Station is conveyed for a distance of 19 yards over an up-and-down road at the Junction entrance, so it can be easily understood that at this point the flow is intense. Immediately beyond, the goods traffic is diverted to the goods yard, where some 28 sidings spread out fanwise, leaving the passenger trains free to flow to the six platform roads and carriage sidings.

Norwich Cathedral.
359

Taken with a Kodak.

With so many seaside resorts close at hand, the excursion traffic in the summer is very heavy, and the ever-popular Yarmouth ranks easily first favourite. On a busy day in the summer Yarmouth claims 10,000 visitors from Norwich. The city is surrounded by a network of junctions, and goods trains flowing from the Ipswich direction are diverted at Upper Junction to the old Victoria Station, which is now used solely for goods traffic and forms an auxiliary goods station in the centre of the City.

At the lower junction the Ipswich and Cambridge main lines meet and proceed through Trowse, where traffic can be diverted via Swing Bridge Junction to the coast or into Thorpe Station.

The movements of traffic in the Passenger Station are controlled from Passenger Yard Box with 125 levers, and goods trains and engines to and from loco. sheds from Goods Yard Box with 62 levers.

In the triangle between Thorpe Junction, Wensum and Swing Bridge Boxes lies Crown Point marshalling yard with its 23 sidings and 5 reception roads. This is built on land utilised for the Royal Show of 1911. It has a working capacity of 500 trucks. During the sugar beet and fishing seasons at Yarmouth and Lowestoft it is a vital factor in the distribution of these commodities.

Norwich can well claim to be self-contained. It has its own loco. depôt, controlling some 200 engines, and is replete with all branches of repair depôts, engineers' works, telegraph, &c.

In the commercial world it ranks foremost in several instances, the chief industry being mustard. The sidings for the mustard works are situated at Trowse, and truck loads are dealt with at that station, the smalls coming into Norwich for forward loading. Wincarnis and Odol have their home in the city, while wire netting, boots and shoes, chocolates, ready-made clothing, all add to the commercial prosperity. An interesting side line is the breeding of Norwich Canaries, which dates back as far as 1713, and it is stated these birds first came over with the Flemish Weavers in the sixteenth century. Some 10,000 birds per annum are sent away all over the world.

In spite of its situation Norwich is well linked up with London by through express trains. There is a daily service to York, and through coaches to Liverpool and Manchester.

The city has a population of 125,000, and is well equipped with public parks and open spaces, and also possesses a private aviation ground, whilst fresh estates built and laid out on modern lines, are springing up on the outskirts.

Dominating the business centre of the city is that lordly pile "The Castle," which radiates, as it were, an influence all its own over the business premises nestling in its shadow.

The Castle, together with the cathedral spire, form landmarks visible for miles around.

If the station is self-contained, so also is the city, with its historic interests, beautiful parks, and educational and commercial activities.

In a word, the "Metropolis of East Anglia" is a city of manifold interest, and one which would well repay a visit.

The London and North Eastern Railway (Southern Area) Building Society.

THE forty-eighth annual meeting of this Society was held in the Board Room at Liverpool Street station on Monday, June 3, the chair being taken by Mr. A. E. Dolden, who was supported by the following directors of the society :—Messrs. A. J. Brickwell, H. G. Drury, G. Farrow, H. H. Maudlin, A. Oldham, and F. V. Russell.

The accounts for the year ended March 31, 1929, which have been prepared in the simplified form approved by the Registrar of Building Societies, indicate that the facilities afforded by the Society to enable members of the staff to acquire their own houses on favourable terms, are being taken advantage of to an increasing extent.

The Society advanced on mortgage during the year £31,696, the total amount due on 501 mortgage securities at the end of the financial year being £153,710.

The shares of the Society form a safe and profitable investment, the amount subscribed during the year being £26,518. Interest is paid at the rate of 4½ per cent., free of income tax.

The membership of the Society increased during the year by 79 to a total of 1,012.

The new rules provide that the auditors shall be appointed by the members of the Society, who accordingly elected for the ensuing year the firm of Messrs. W. B. Peat & Co.

Members of the staff desiring to join the Society, either as borrowers or investors, may obtain a copy of the prospectus or balance-sheet from the secretary Mr. E. J. Hills, Room 119, Hamilton House, Liverpool Street Station, London.

The Railway Age (U.S.A.) endeavours to explain to its readers the new meaning given to the word "rationalisation" :—

"If a railroad ceases to function entirely by force of habit ; if it examines its operations critically, finds their flaws and reorganises its processes, in the light of its studies, to improve its efficiency—that is 'rationalisation.' It is a word and an idea which has achieved enormous popularity in Europe in the past few years."

Key to photographs on next page.

The Canning Industry at Lowestoft.

By F. G. G. COBB, District Goods and Passenger Manager's Office, Norwich.

THE progress of science carries in its train revolutionary changes affecting every aspect of life. This is strikingly evident to-day in the world of travel, of industry, and of amusement. It is also particularly noticeable in modern domestic life. There is an amazing contrast between the conditions under which the modern housewife lives and those in existence in the days of her mediæval sister. We cannot but regard with satisfaction the rapid advance made in recent years resulting in multitudinous conveniences and facilities being placed at the disposal of the housewife of to-day. Not the least important of her duties is the catering for the household, and there is little doubt that the production and marketing of canned fish, fruit and vegetables, which provide epicurian and seasonal table delicacies at all times of the year, have done much to lighten the task and widen the choice. These canned commodities also take pride of place at picnics, broadland and other increasingly popular holidays.

To meet the growing demand a well-known firm has recently erected an extensive modern-equipped cannery on property rented from the London & North Eastern Railway at Lowestoft South Side, which with other old-established canneries at Lowestoft cater for the country's requirements in the shape of canned fish, pastes, tongues, beef, soup, and peas to the extent of 5,000 tons per annum, the majority of which passes via the London & North Eastern Railway.

The canneries, which are self-contained except for manufacturing the glass receptacles, make their own cans from tin plates drawn from South Wales tin mines at the rate of 1,700 tons per annum. The scrap metal is baled and sold, some 400 tons being despatched to London and other places by rail yearly.

They are divided into numerous spacious and hygienic preparing rooms, each with its staff of spotless overalled girls, its special machinery, and its foodstuffs the quality of which would appeal to any gastronomic individual and give the lie to the old gag "They eat what they can and 'can' what they can't."

They are connected by sidings with the London & North Eastern Railway, and have a water frontage that permits of fresh herrings being virtually whisked from the sea to the can; 4,500,000 are canned annually at Lowestoft. Fishing vessels unload their catches at the fish preparing rooms, ensuring perfect condition and obviating boxing in ice or salt, handling in the market and cartage. The fish is beheaded, gutted, pickled for 20 minutes, washed in huge rotary machines and afterwards deftly curled up in oval-shaped cans on a bed of rich tomato, the lids of the cans being fixed by machinery at the rate of 1,800 per hour. They are then packed on trays and placed in immense steam controlled retorts registering 230 deg. F. for 1½ hours to cook and sterilise the contents, after which time they are taken out and stabbed with lightning rapidity to release the hot air and moisture, the holes being soldered immediately afterwards to seal the cans hermetically. Then follows a night in the cooling rooms, tests for faulty tins, washing, lacquering, labelling and boxing. Soups are prepared and cans filled by machinery.

Lambs', calves' and ox tongues, briskets of beef and other meats enjoy the comfort of glass containers which are thoroughly cleaned before being used. Some 400 tons pass annually in their raw state from London and Liverpool to Lowestoft by rail. They are cleaned and pickled in vats for periods varying from four to 14 days. The containers are filled and the caps and rings fixed under a pressure of 800 lb. Cooking and sterilising is done in the same manner as the herrings except that greater care has to be exercised, the maximum temperature of 212 being reached by varying degrees and the temperature gradually lowered before opening the retort doors, otherwise the rush of cold air would crack the glasses.

The most popular lines produced are fish and meat pastes. The ingredients are cooked and spiced, then ground by special machinery which automatically fills the glass containers at the rate of 15,000 per day, after which they, too, have to be sterilised in a temperature of 220 deg. F.

The only vegetables prepared are peas, which are grown mostly in Lincolnshire, and are brought to Lowestoft by rail during the month of July at the rate of four tons per day.

A conservative estimate of the number of tins turned out at Lowestoft annually is given as 9,000,000.

The well-known firm of Maconochie Brothers, who created the memorable war ration, are not now canning at Lowestoft. Their output during the Great War has never been equalled, but the present industrial outlook in the canning industry induces the Lowestoft manufacturers to hope that ere long they will exceed that tonnage under far more peaceful circumstances.

(Key to photographs, page 20.)

1. Scotch girls gutting.
2. A typical Lowestoft Cannery.
3. Fishing vessels. One arriving with herrings, the other leaving after unloading catch.
4. A display of Lowestoft products.

Great Eastern Goat Society.

As there has been no membership of this society for the past two years, the vice-presidents agreed to the winding up of its affairs. They also agreed the balance in hand, amounting to £5 2s. 2d., be sent as a donation to the funds of the Railway Convalescent Homes.

In regard to the challenge cups; the vice-presidents decided these should remain in the possession of the present holders, but were not to be considered their absolute property. In the event of the society being revived at some future date, the cups to be made available for competition among members.

The silver cup presented by the late Lord Claud Hamilton, the first president of the society, is held by Mr. Grimes, stationmaster, North Elmham, and the vice-president's cup by Mr. Wybrew, stationmaster, Audley End.

Book Notices.

ESSAYS OF A LOCOMOTIVE MAN. By E. A. Phillipson. 5½ in. by 8½ in.; 143 pages. Published by the Locomotive Publishing Co. Ltd., Amen Corner, E.C.4. 3s. 6d. Although the author apologises somewhat profusely for the "dubious use" he has made of the English language, the language he uses is very much more understandable than that usually to be found in a book dealing with such abstruse matters as "design ratios," and will, we think, be thoroughly enjoyed by those whose knowledge of locomotives is not bounded by their wheel formation. There are 35 essays in all reprinted from *The Locomotive* (guarantee of quality), and as they are admittedly on argumentative subjects, mutual improvement class members and others will doubtless revel in the book.

BRITISH LOCOMOTIVES. By G. Gibbard Jackson. 5½ in. by 9 in. by 1½ in. Published by Sampson Low & Co. Ltd., 6s. net, is still another book for the locomotive lover, and will serve admirably as a gift. It is not easy to resist a volume containing well over 100 pictures of engines and 246 pages of gossip about them. Who would have thought that the cab originated through some boys dropping a brick from an overbridge, or that the old drivers objected to the cab because they had been "used to the open air and hated the confinement of same "?

A GUIDE TO PRIVATE SIDING PROBLEMS: RAILWAY RATES AND CHARGES. By William Oldham. Published by the Industrial Transport Publications Limited. Ninety pages of solid instruction on what the publishers with some reason call "an abstruse and contentious subject." A really valuable book.

21

QUAINT BUILDINGS AND STREETS OF NORWICH

By F. G. G. COBB, District Goods and Passenger
Manager's Office, Norwich

NORWICH is so rich with antiquity, so overpoweringly mediæval, " more so even than either York, Chester or Bristol," that the full story of its ancient possessions or a complete description of its quaint streets, cobbled alleyways and gabled houses beloved of artists, will never be told. Every street is redolent of the middle ages with its rows of mediæval buildings still with the old door knockers, the heads of Queen Anne, the lions of the first Georges, the straps of the fourth William and many scores of Grocers' Arms that, like the City's great girdle of walls, are significant of its former greatness.

Modernity expresses itself in the imposing masonry and brickwork of the City's business houses and factories, but the stranger can well obtain a feast of antiquarian delight by turning down the many narrow alleyways and passages, where, tucked away with apparently squalid dwelling-houses, are fine Tudor and Georgian structures, beautiful oaken doorways with carved lintels that oft-times framed some fair Flemish maiden whilst her parents within plied at their trade of weaving that made the City so prosperous in the fifteenth and sixteenth centuries.

A beautiful picture of Elm Hill is reproduced. The Corporation of Norwich has acquired the whole of the property and are gradually restoring it in accordance with the period.

Meandering down the steep decline cobbled with the original stone is like stepping right into the middle ages, the wanderer feeling that he should have a cloak to cover the modernity of his clothing and a periwig to hide his harsh poll. An old thatched public house, displaying the sign of the Britons' Arms, commands an uninterrupted view down the winding hill. Conjecture has it that it was once the residence of the prior of the Bishop of Hungate, whose fane still stands at the top of the hill in a state of disuse.

Many a procession has been viewed from the windows of that overhanging upper storey, the famous weavers' pageant held when Queen Elizabeth visited Norwich to take toll of her loyal and loving citizens, and many a time has Sir John Paston, famous for the Paston Letters of the fifteenth century, passed by from his town house a little further down the street to the Church that he rebuilt and to whom we are now indebted for a remarkable timbered roof, fine glass windows and two oaken doors coveted by some of our American visitors.

A few steps on the left a mediæval door with a tiny grill about the height of one's head, through which the porter would scrutinise all callers before admitting them into the courtyard beyond, then, abutting, a fourteenth century house completely restored in accordance with the period. This is where Paston lived. Prior to 1545 it was occupied by Augustine Steward, whose merchant mark appears with the arms of the Mercers' Company on a beautifully carved beam across the entrance to what is called Crown Court. Many interesting relics have been revealed in the course of restoration, including a fine Tudor ceiling and an interesting sixteenth century fireplace. It is now " The Strangers Club," and many gatherings are held in the long upper storey room that extends the full length of the building.

On the other side of the street stands the seventeenth century Samson and Hercules House that has several features of historic interest. Two huge wooden figures stand sentinel on either side of the doorway and give a striking effect to its front, which is in keeping with its immediate neighbour, Augustine Steward's house, built in the reign of Henry VIII, that now houses the bric-à-brac of an antique dealer. It has the merchant's mark of Augustine Steward, a former Mayor of the City, still visible on a corner bracket. It was Augustine Steward who gave to the City of Norwich the mace made of polished pieces of rock crystal set in silver gilt that can still be seen with the priceless civic regalia in the Guildhall and is still used on certain civic occasions. The mace is one of the most beautiful in England and only one other like it is known in Europe.

One must awaken from a delightful reverie to find that only a few yards of bottled history have been explored. The visitor can ramble in every direction and enrich and link up his modern imagination with the spirits of the past.

The Merchants' houses, Strangers Hall, Suckling House, Curats House and the Bridewell are all open to the public, the Music House, a remarkable survival of a Jew's House of the twelfth century equal to any of its period, of which only five or six remain in the country, the Old Barge Inn, a glorious old fourteenth century house, the wealth of Churches so essentially Flemish, that possess ecclesiastic treasures unsurpassed throughout the land, and many other buildings, all help to make Norwich the City of a thousand memories.

180

Photo.]
Elm Hill, Norwich
[W. B. Driffield, A.R.P.S.

181

CROMER AND THE CRAB FISHING INDUSTRY

By F. G. G. COBB, District Goods and Passenger Manager's Office, Norwich

FRESH-WATER and estuarine deposits belonging to the Forest Bed series, the remains of huge extinct mammals, including the hippopotamus, cave bear, sabre-toothed tiger, and three species of elephants, have been discovered in the cliffs at Cromer, where a large river, probably the Rhine, once flowed. There is evidence which suggests that part of England was at one time connected with the mainland of Europe, but since then the sea has gradually gained an ascendancy.

During the reign of Henry IV (1399-1413) the countryside in Great Britain that offers endless opportunities for delightful excursions, and is served by the fastest express trains on the Eastern Section of the Southern Area of the L. & N.E.R.

The easily accessible beach has a wealth of natural resources. Even the staple industry of crab fishing provides an entertainment, a chance to haul the crab boats ashore and to gather speculatively around the baskets alive with the finest fish food extant.

Crab fishing is carried on along the North

Typical Old Salts

town of Shipden, in which parish Cromer was then situated, was swallowed by the sea. In recent years thousands of tons of cliff on either side of the town (safely away from visitors) has thundered to the shore to be pounded flat by the ever-encroaching North Sea, and Cromer itself probably owes its very existence to a huge sea wall erected in 1894.

Cromer is the ideal holiday resort. Its hotels, boarding houses and shops are the acme of modernity, whilst a link with past ages is reflected in the fine old fourteenth century church of SS. Peter and Paul. It dominates the centre of the town and seems to preserve the quiet dignity of a cathedral city.

The town stands on the edge of cliffs between 100 and 200 feet in height, midst the most beautiful

Norfolk coast from Salthouse to Happisburgh (local appellation Hasboro) for a distance of 20 miles. Statistics issued by the Ministry of Fisheries shows that in recent years the most productive year was in 1926, when 1,899,000 saleable crabs were landed in the district. The yield in 1929 was just under a million crabs and the value just under £10,000. The minimum legal size of a crab that can be landed is 4¼ in., and the marketing is at a price "per hundred," which actually represents 240 crabs.

Altogether on the North Norfolk coast there are 19 motor boats and 47 sailing craft tending nearly 10,000 pots during the season, which extends from March to September. The pots are baited with garnets or plaice caught at Lowestoft and dropped

480

Lowering the baited
crab pot to the bed
of the ocean

The Beach Inspector
who measures the
crab to ensure con-
formity to minimum
size regulations

into the sea on a "shank" any distance from the shore up to between three and four miles out. A "shank" is a long rope to which 40 pots are attached, each about 20 feet from the other. They are lowered to the ocean bed, a buoy being fixed at each end to acquaint the fishermen of their whereabouts. There they remain until the following morning, when they are hauled up, emptied into baskets, re-baited and again lowered into the sea, the boats returning to the shore with the crabs and the incoming tide.

It is a strenuous job pulling up those brine-sodden ropes and hauling the heavy iron-bottomed pots

into the frail tossing surf boats, but the fishermen of Cromer are born to the sea and hazard more when they ride tremendous seas in the lifeboat that stands on the end of the pier ever ready to answer a signal of distress.

The harvest is bigger in mild weather. When it is cold the crabs bury themselves in the sand and remain there. A large percentage are cooked and sold to visitors and residents, and 100 tons are despatched alive by passenger train, the principal receiving stations being Norwich, Yarmouth, Lowestoft and Cambridge.

481

209

"FISHERGATE, NORWICH"

By F. G. G. COBB, District Goods and Passenger Manager's Office, Norwich

WHEN Albert, patriarch of Jerusalem, instituted the Carmelites or White Friars at Mount Carmel in Syria, in A.D. 1200, he endowed Norwich with historical interests that will live with posterity. The order spread over the world, and in A.D. 1268 the religious monastery of White Friars was founded in Fishergate by Philip Cowgate, a rich merchant and mayor of the City, "who when he had made an end of the fabrick thereof which he endowed with fair possessions, took upon himself the habit and order of a Carmelite and entered the house and ended his days."

Fishergate means "the street of the fishermen," and imagination can well visualise the tall peak-roofed houses on either side of the narrow cobbled street in the first blush of their youth housing the fishermen in the middle and later centuries who landed their fish from the river which runs lazily past the back of their houses on the south side. One can also picture the animated scenes at the mediæval fish stalls almost at the walls of the Priory of the Carmelites, in whose fine church were buried citizens of note, including Dame Margery Paston, whose epistles to her husband John Paston are the most interesting of "The Paston Letters," and the quietude of the Sabbath in those days broken only by the clatter of feet on the cobblestones as the fishermen and their families passed on their way to the Church of St. Edmunds, where amongst the precious relics greatly reverenced was a piece of the shirt of St. Edmund the Martyr, preserved in a crystal box.

In Fishergate to-day modernity is jealously hanging on to its links with past ages. Close to White Friars Bridge, a modern stone structure, a piece of flint and stone wall bearing an ancient inscription that has been carefully propped up, is the last relic of the ancient Priory, but the Church of St. Edmunds still stands although the piece of shirt has long since vanished without a clue.

The ancient fane is now only used as a Sunday school, and the churchyard is completely overgrown with weeds, save where some immense stones mark the resting places of past benefactors. Its ecclesiastic tranquility is disturbed by the incessant click, click, click of machines in adjacent boot-making factories, but the lover of architecture can well restore his ecstatic inspiration by gazing across the road at the ancient half-timbered, peak-roofed houses that have been so splendidly reproduced on the front page of this issue.

It is indeed a feast for the antiquarian, for the buildings have magnificently weathered the long tumultuous years, the devasting Black Plague and the fire of 1591, when the Fish Stalls were burned and erected again. The deeds of the "Tiger Inn" date back to 1601, but for many years previous the buildings must have graced the thoroughfare and conjecture has it they formed part of the conventual buildings of the monastery before Henry VIII dissolved it in 1548.

At the extreme right of the picture the opening leads to a tiny courtyard, fringed with somewhat squalid dwellings, and one cannot help wondering whether or not cynicism prompted the authority who named it "The Staff of Life Yard."

CASUALTY FUND, RAILWAY BENEVOLENT INSTITUTION

NEW YEAR'S DAY COLLECTION, 1933

THE customary New Year's Day collection for the Casualty Fund of the Railway Benevolent Institution will be made at all stations on Monday, January 2, 1933, and it is hoped that every railway employee (including women) will become members of the Casualty Fund for 1933 by subscribing the sum of 1s., which entitles the member, should occasion arise, to participate in the following benefits, irrespective of means from other sources :—

Accidental death	£5 to widow* : if no widow,* £3 to orphans. If single, £3 to next-of-kin.
Accidental injury	Donation according to period of absence from work, of about 3s. 6d. per week.
Ordinary death ...	£4 to widow* (or widower).

* In the case of women subscribers, read "widower" in place of widow.

During the present year no fewer than 168,626 have become members of the Fund, and assistance has already been rendered in a large number of cases.

The Casualty Fund may be regarded as a valuable insurance against injury or death. The method of claiming is of the simplest character, and every application is dealt with immediately upon receipt.

Whilst we understand that in many places almost the entire staff secure for themselves membership by the payment of the 1/- subscription, it is felt that there are certain shops, depots and stations where the value of membership is not sufficiently appreciated, and that if the advantages of the Casualty Fund were brought more prominently to their notice, few would fail to subscribe.

THE ROMANCE OF NORFOLK CYDER MAKING

By F. G. G. COBB, District Goods and Passenger Manager's Office, Norwich

OFT-TIMES in the middle of last century when the mantle of night had spread over the peaceful little village of Banham, Norfolk, the quiet solitude would be broken by the cluttering of a horse and trolley as it passed through the solitary street. The driver was Mr. William Gaymer, son of a farmer of repute whose parents had for generations past made cyder in the quiet seclusion of the village. He was taking the product of his father to the colleges at Cambridge, where it was in great demand.

Exactly when cyder making was first introduced into the village is not known. It is an ancient art whose origin is lost in antiquity. The inhabitants of Normandy crushed the harvests of their apple orchards into wine before the twelfth century, and it was brought to England in the early part of that period. There were, and still are, flourishing orchards in Banham and it is not at all singular that soon after it should be recorded that "the Lord of the Manor (at Banham) had apple orchards reckoned at three casks of cyder (dolia Cysarica) price of a cask 10s."

The ancient recipe was handed down from generation to generation, and it has been left to Mr. William Gaymer to develop the heritage to such an extent that the wine is now a household word appreciated throughout the world, and the business occupies extensive and up-to-date works with siding accommodation at our Attleborough Station, some five miles from Banham, with a staff of nearly 300, and a London branch where nearly 100 are employed. Instead of the modest horse and trolley, special trains convey the firm's output during the hot weather to Whitemoor and the North, also London and the South; the daily loadings have reached a maximum of 87 wagons and the total annual tonnage of inwards and outwards traffics approximates 3,000 tons.

On January 9, 1933, Mr. Gaymer celebrated his ninety-first birthday. He is a senior director of Messrs. Gaymer & Sons Ltd., and spent his birthday as usual at the imposing Head Offices which stand as a monument to his life's endeavours.

The story of the early struggles and the epic of labour involved in the realisation of an ideal cannot be dealt with here, and I must content myself with a brief outline of the industry which is as closely allied to the Railway as any business in the country, for not only is all the very considerable output of cyder distributed throughout the world, via the London & North-Eastern Railway, but the empty casks, cases, bottles are returned, and apples, new bottles, and every other commodity employed in the manufacture are conveyed by the same method of transportation.

The dull, sour, still cyder of the ancient days has now been replaced by a brilliant beverage, but the basis for the production is the same as of yore, except that modern science has now allied itself to practical experience, and bacteriology, biology, botany, and agriculture have all contributed in effecting improvements in the production of fruit suitable for cyder making and the control of the fermentive, maturing and bottling processes.

The ultimate quality of cyder depends largely on the best selection of apples grown in suitable soil and harvested at the right time, and great care is used to see that only sound fruit is used, as over-ripe apples favour the growth of moulds which impart a musty flavour to the juice.

Fruit not only from Norfolk, but the great apple-growing counties of Cambridge, Kent, Somerset, Devon and Gloucestershire, are brought into our Attleborough Station for Messrs. Gaymer to the extent of several thousand tons every season, which extends from September to December.

The first impressions of a visit to the works are the kindness and courtesy of the officials, the well-ordered cleanliness throughout (even the factory walls are faced with well-pruned pear trees), and the bewildering rows of huge wooden vats in the maturing rooms that rise to the roofs of the buildings like the "utmost towers of Ilium" and dwarf the workmen beneath. Many vats hold 25,000 gallons of cyder, but even these fade into insignificance when compared with the latest types of containers which are gradually replacing them. They are really great concrete rooms, the whole of the interior covered with a tasteless and innocuous lining, and built in solid blocks of about six, the uppermost being reached by staircases resembling ship's ladders. Each block has a total capacity of approximately 150,000 gallons.

The selected apples are stored at the top of the main building, dropped through shoots into roller mills on the floor below and crushed into pulp by spiked cylindrical drums at the rate of 100 tons a day. The pulp is conveyed to hydraulic presses where the juice is extracted. Manilla cloths are filled with the pulp and the sides and ends folded like an envelope. These are placed on the top of each other with the folds uppermost and the juice forced through by hydraulic pressure to trays beneath from whence it is pumped to fermentation vats.

The most careful technical control of the fermentation is necessary, otherwise the final liquor is unattractive. The whole process follows the lines of the practice in the grape-wine-producing countries, and fragrant ethers develop in cyder precisely in the same way as champagne. Certain vinous secondary products are produced which give characteristic bouquet and flavour. The fermented juice is passed through filtering machinery and finally passed to the bottling stage. One cannot

machines with an output of over 100 dozen per hour. It is sufficient to state that this Champagne of England, produced as it is in the centre of the Norfolk turkey industry, is an all-British product throughout.

Loading

cyder at

Gaymer's siding,

Attleborough, Norfolk

The first special train loaded with Gaymer's cyder bound for White-moor and beyond

dwell at length upon the up-to-date machinery, which includes automatic hydro-washers that cleanse and rinse several hundred dozen bottles every hour, and a very extensive bottling plant including filling

The honour of a Royal Warrant of Appointment to H.M. The King which was granted some years ago has recently been supplemented with a Warrant of Appointment to H.R.H. The Prince of Wales.

137

212

A PEEP AT CARROW WORKS, NORWICH

By F. G. G. COBB, District Goods and Passenger Manager's Office, Norwich

WHATEVER commentaries may be made upon the adventurous spirit of the modern business youth, it is logical to refer to the outstanding ideals and attainments of our ancestors and to the flourishing industries which survive them and stand as monuments to their pioneer grit. Not the least of these is Messrs. J. & J. Colman, Ltd., mustard manufacturers, Norwich, which firm's

and by constantly improving his machinery was able to produce in turn a "fine" and "superfine" flour. The business developed so rapidly that in 1856 it was removed to its present site at Carrow Works, Norwich.

To take an impression of a tiny water mill on a visit to the works, or to dwell on the epic of labour that lay in the construction and development of

Photograph]   [Swain, St. Giles, Norwich

Mustard Reaping

progress marks the greatest evolution in East Anglian commercial history.

In 1814, a Mr. Jeremiah Colman took over a water mill in Stoke Holy Cross, a tiny village near Norwich, and decided to make mustard. He was not the first to discover the efficacy of the mustard seed itself. Credit for this was given to Æsculapius, the god of Medicine, by the ancient Greeks, and it is well known that its value was appreciated from the earliest times, the Romans probably being responsible for spreading its fame over Europe. Since that time references to the tiny seed are constantly occurring in the pages of English literature. Mr. Jeremiah Colman was not content with the crude coarse production of that period,

the industry from those early days of the solitary mill to the present wealth of buildings, eloquent of steady and substantial progress, would be simply asking for a temporary disturbance of mental poise, for not only is the world-renowned Colman's mustard — now "double-superfine" — manufactured, but in all fifteen different articles in addition to subsidiary products. To name a few—starch, blue, cornflour, self-raising flour, Waverley oats, semolina, and products of Keen Robinson & Co., a firm amalgamated with Messrs. Colman since 1903, Robinson's "Patent" barley, Robinson's groats, and Keen's complete food "Almata."

Visitors to Norwich can catch a glimpse of the sidings that connect the works with our Trowse

An Aerial View of Carrow Works

station, and as their train passes over the swing bridge a few yards distant, can see an almost unbroken line of tall buildings with excellent water-transport facilities, stretching for the greater part of a mile along the bank of the river Wensum; but a real impression of the enormous "power" of the enterprise is gained from viewing it, as was my privilege, from the roof of the highest building in the centre of the works.

I looked on a remarkable diversity of scenery. Around me were more than fifty acres of closely built factories throbbing with machinery, railway lines ribboning their way between blocks of buildings with refreshing intimacy, and tiny engines pulling trucks in the yards below. The river Wensum wound itself lazily past one side and disappeared into a vista of natural picturesqueness, the richly-wooded estate of Mr. Russell Colman, named Crown Point, where the last Royal Show was held in Norwich in 1911. Behind me the Norman spire of the Norwich Cathedral pierced the sky.

It is impossible to make a thorough tour of the works even in a day, and my guide pointed out to me some of the buildings time would not permit of a visit. The electric power house, which supplies both power and light for the whole works. The steam plant, where over sixty thousand gallons of water are converted every day into steam for heating the buildings and to provide "fuel" for Gamma and Delta, the two steam engines without furnaces, that haul railway wagons to and from our Trowse station. These engines are charged with 200 lb. pressure of steam every six hours and have a maximum hauling power of twenty loaded wagons. (A few feet away from the steam plant are the lovely gardens of Carrow Abbey, belonging to the Colman family, where the workers wander during their lunch hour in the summer time.) Then the printing works where every year hundreds of tons of paper (and tons of ink) are turned into leaflets, circulars, menus, colour work and labels by the millions. Deals and battens from the Balkans stacked high in the wood yards next the saw mills and wood box departments, where batteries of machines convert thousands of tons of wood into printed boxes every year. The "Almata" factory, where the complete food for infants and invalids is made under scientific and hygienic conditions, and the flour, barley and groats mills rearing their heads higher than the rest. The Blue Mill near the river, which brings along in barges the ultramarine for the making of those little cubes or cylinders which are produced at the rate of 21,000 per machine per hour, known the whole world over as "blue bags." The Administrative Offices, which are connected by a private telephone line with the London offices, and which house nearly 200 men and women; the kitchens which

One of the Tin Box Department Floors

192

215

Loading up in Carrow Works

provide the staff with meals at purely nominal prices; the club house and bowling greens and, besides many other places of interest, the surgery and rest house, where a hospital nurse and doctor are available for any of the 2,000 employees.

In the mustard mill I learned there are many varieties of mustard seed, but for practical purposes only two of these have to be considered, the brown and white varieties otherwise known as *sinapis nigra* and *sinapis alba*. Of these, the former requires a peculiarly rich soil for its cultivation, and this is found chiefly in the alluvial marshlands. Suffolk, Norfolk, Cambridgeshire, Lincolnshire and Yorkshire are the best mustard-growing districts.

The seed is drilled in March or April and grows very quickly, the plants reaching a height of six feet or more when they flower in June. The yellow blossom covering acre after acre is one of the chief beauties of the fen country. The flowers fall giving place to seed pods, and in August the crop is harvested. When the seed arrives at the mill it is first of all graded. The secret of accurate grading and of calculating from this the exact proportions in which the two seeds must be combined is one which has been handed down from generation to generation and is still jealously guarded. After cleaning and sorting processes

the white and brown seeds are milled separately, the brown having to go through a greater number of stages than the white. Powerful rollers grind many tons of seed every year, and after varying processes of sifting, this is finally shaken through fine sieves that have 20,000 holes to the square inch. Perhaps readers will pause to consider the texture of the silk material that is used. At each stage of the conversion from seed to flour there are certain residues which are scientifically converted into such by-products as mustard bran for hydropathic purposes and mustard cake for use as a fertiliser. The mixing of the two flours from the brown and white seeds takes place in hoppers which each have a capacity of one and a half tons. In some grades a little wheat flour is added to give the consistency which accords with English taste. Before being conveyed to the packing floors, the mustard is sifted once again to complete the mixing.

The machines in the mustard packing departments are ingenious and fascinating. An endless and long procession of tins and lids, three and four deep, passes slowly through a machine which fills, weighs and fits the lids on over 3,000 each hour, and then continues on its way to another machine, that by dexterously turning over each tin plugs on the label and returns it to the procession which winds along to the packers ready to place the tins in wooden cases for their journey to almost every part of the globe.

The tin box department is equally entertaining to the visitor. Sheets of tin which arrive in bundles from South Wales at the rate of thousands of tons every year, are converted into tins by a succession of machines. Some are made as quickly as 250 per minute, and every week hundreds of thousands of them with their lids radiate on endless belts running through holes in the walls of the department to the various packing departments. The furthest is the barley mill over one hundred yards away, which is connected by an electrically-lighted tunnel running right through the flour mill. Four continuous bands run through the tunnel and

combined consignment note, invoice and account form in sets which comprise :

(1) Firm's note for warehouseman and copy of consignment note.

(2) Copy of note required for rendering by the firm to their London house.

(3) L.N.E.R. account.

(4) Combined consignment note, copy of invoice and copy of account.

(5) Railway invoice which, of course, is sent forward with the goods.

These are charged out by two railway clerks permanently employed within the works. During last year a total of 100,000 sets were used, which embraced 20,350 tons of traffic for which 9,700

Road Motor Service at Norwich

upon these are conveyed decorated tins in which the barley is packed. It takes eight minutes for each tin to pass through.

I passed into the starch mill where rice, which comes mainly from British possessions in the East, is softened, ground and converted into blocks containing 47 per cent. of water; saw the huge ovens where the blocks spend varying periods at different temperatures until the formation of those crystals with which every housewife is familiar. I was intrigued by the remarkable machines that quickly transform huge rolls of paper into printed boxes, and others that fill them with starch, weigh and seal over 4,000 in an hour, the movements being impossible to detect with the naked eye.

To the railwayman, the evidence of close co-operation is very refreshing. Messrs. J. & J. Colman employ their own loaders and issue their own

wagons were used, an average of thirty-eight each working day. 3,400 loaded wagons, an average of fourteen each working day, were worked into the factory from our Trowse station in the same period.

A recent development has been the conveyance of grain from farms to the mills throughout by our own motor lorries, one consignment worthy of note weighing 127 tons and involving a total journey of 180 miles.

The predominant impressions of a short tour are the enormity of the works, the great diversity of output, the super-machinery, the courtesy and cheerfulness of the staff, cleanliness, the complete absence of hustle, and Gamma and Delta for ever hauling our trucks containing the output of a perfectly controlled organisation which symbolises the perfection of a master miller's ideal.

194

THE NORWICH ROSE INDUSTRY

By F. COBB, District Goods and Passenger Manager's Office, Norwich

OVER one million rose bushes were collected by our lorries from the rose nurseries of Messrs. Ernest Morse & Son, Eaton, Norwich and safely delivered to Messrs. Woolworth's branch stores in all parts of the British Isles during October and November last year.

have grown roses and have left as evidence of a steady industry ideal nurseries that slope gently to a most delightful river and countryside.

There are many acres of glasshouse where tomatoes and cucumbers are produced, but the principal features are the folds of roses at this

What visions can be conjured if we muse over this for a moment! The Irishman planting a rose in Erin's soil, the Scotsman buying one for saxpence; crowded stores and the contrasting tranquillity of the garden; summer time and glorious blooms that owe their existence to the care they received just without the ancient walls of the City of Norwich where millions more are now being nurtured for next season's distribution.

For centuries past the forbears of Messrs. Morse

nursery and at Cringleford, near Norwich, covering 300 acres.

Until the imposition of tariffs on rose bushes from Holland about four years ago, the production of roses by this firm was quite a modest industry, and only 12 men were needed in this branch of their business. It has now reached enormous proportions, requiring the employment of over 150 men and girls and involving extensions in land and buildings.

It actually takes three years to produce a rose bush for marketing. Cuttings, called stocks, are taken from wild roses in November and are transplanted a year later. Budding takes place in June of the next year. The bushes bloom for the first time in the following summer and are sold in October and November of that year.

Messrs. Morse & Son import two and a half million one-year-old wild rose stocks from Holland in November.

The stocks are planted six inches apart in rows two feet eight inches distant. This distance between the rows is wider than is the common practice, and permits of the use of large horse hoes which hoe four rows at a time. The saving of labour by this means of cultivation more than compensates for the additional land occupied and gives a very marked improvement in the size and quality of the rose bushes. The total length of the rows is about 250 miles.

Planting is done by men and girls who work in pairs. The man digs a hole, and the girl, who carries a bundle of stocks in her arm, plants one in the hole, the man pressing the soil round the stock with his foot.

From November to June the land is carefully cultivated. The stocks by this time have become firmly established, are in full leaf and ready for budding. This operation is the most delicate and important part of the rose grower's business and is carried out with the skill and precision of a medical surgeon. A razor-shape knife with a special ivory tip is used. A perpendicular cut is made in the bark up the main short stem and at the top a cross cut forming the shape of a T. The bark is then easily lifted and the eye of a cultivated English rose placed in the incision with the tip of the budding knife. The eye for this purpose is taken from the variety of rose intended for reproduction and is found growing at the junction between the main stem and the leaf. The leaf is removed from the shoot leaving approximately $\frac{1}{4}$-inch of stalk, and the eye complete with its surrounding bark is then shaved off. Great care is used to cut just the bark containing the eye, and any hard wood adhering to the bark is removed. The bark of the wild rose stock is then put back to its original position and, holding the inserted rose eye in position, the wound is carefully bound with raffia to prevent the stock from drying up. The raffia lasts sufficiently long to enable the eye to make growing contact with its wild foster-parent. This work is carried out with remarkable rapidity. Budding finishes about the first week in September when the employees are given a week's holiday before starting the important task of lifting the bushes that were budded the previous year.

These are all lifted by spade, brought from the fields to the packing sheds by motor lorries, where the roots are firmly mossed and a label the same colour as the rose and bearing the name of the plant is affixed to each. They are then tied in bundles of ten and packed in wooden crates, each holding 250 to 500 bushes.

In recent years the firm has adopted various improved methods of packing and have increased their daily output from 12,000 in 1932, to 40,000 at the end of last year. When the new packing sheds now in course of erection are completed this number is expected to be increased to 80,000 bushes.

The crates are lined with brown paper and the lids fixed by a wire banding machine. Messrs. Morse & Son claim many advantages for this method over the usual practice of packing in hay. It takes approximately 25 minutes to pack 250 rose bushes in hay, the package is often 10 to 12 feet in length requiring two men to carry it, and has been known to arrive at its destination in halves. The wooden crates, although more costly, can be packed in a fraction of this time, are less liable to damage, and can be easily handled.

The whole output is carted by our motor lorries to Norwich Thorpe Station for despatch by rail, and at the conclusion of last season our Agent received a letter of thanks that is worthy of reproduction—

" Now that we have completed our shipment of rose trees for the season to Messrs. F. W. Woolworth & Co. Ltd., we feel we must write to thank you for the very kind co-operation which you have given us. We realised that October and November are quite busy months for you, and we know that sometimes it must have meant quite a lot of thinking out to arrange for the five lorries to come after our consignments each day; and if it did, we must additionally thank you for the kind way in which you refrained from ever mentioning it to us."

It is an interesting fact that the soil on which the roses are grown is of comparatively poor quality. Experiments have proved that roses taken from such soil not only make more fibrous roots in their search for moisture, but thrive far better when transplanted than those produced in richer soil.

The millions of blooms in the summer lend added charm to the countryside, and on one Saturday in each year called "The Ernest Morse and Son Annual Rose Day," they give colour to the City of Norwich and revenue to local hospitals. On this day over 100,000 are sold in the streets and practically everybody wears one. They are given by Messrs. Morse & Son, who conceived the idea and voluntarily organise the whole distribution. By their efforts over £2,000 has been collected in five years.

200

219

Crates of rose bushes ready for despatch

[Photograph]   [Nassau

A group of Morse and Son's employees

201

VOL. 27   No. 7

JULY, 1937

London & North Eastern
Railway Magazine

ON THE NORFOLK BROADS

Photograph by Charles E. Brown, London.

375

THE NORFOLK BROADLAND
By F. Cobb, District Goods and Passenger Manager's Office, Norwich

WHEN the sea receded from the walls of the ancient City of Norwich in the dim and distant past, it left for this present age a charming heritage of tortuous rivers and expansive broads that are the resort of thousands of holiday makers, and flat country to which the passing years have added a quaint picturesqueness and alluring beauty, much of which, with its windmills and dykes, bears a striking resemblance to scenery in Holland.

interests in Broadland, of the charming reaches, ancient chain ferries and ferryhouses, ruined abbeys on its banks, the broadland churches, the keen sense of exhilaration when running close-hauled in one of the thousand or more yachts that can be hired ; of the pride of steering a hired motor cruiser which probably cost nearly a thousand pounds, and is yours for a week or fortnight.

The largest of the rivers is the Yare, which flows

On the Broads
Photograph by Charles E. Brown

There are 200 miles of navigable waterways, principally the rivers Yare, Waveney and the Bure, with its tributaries the Thurne and the Ant and about 50 vast expanses of water called Broads, connected with the rivers in most instances by long reed-fringed dykes that pass through meadows rich with wild-fowl, wild iris and other flora. It is the most diverting experience cruising along these narrow dykes in a yacht or motor launch, or rowing in a small boat, and suddenly finding oneself on a fine sheet of water about 100 acres in extent.

It would take volumes to tell of the diversity of

from Norwich to Yarmouth and has boating centres at Norwich, Brundall and Reedham. This is commercially the most important, and is used by huge trading vessels plying between the Continent and other places and the Port of Norwich. It is a strange sight on this river to see an old-time sailing wherry dwarfing numerous small sailing yachts, being passed by a modern luxury motor cruiser, with a diesel-engined sea-going cargo vessel following in its wake.

The real charm and peacefulness of the Norfolk Broads is to be found on the rivers Waveney and

376

Bure. On May 22 members of the Liverpool Street Headquarters Staff took a steamer trip from Yarmouth to St. Olaves on the river Waveney across the wide salt estuary Breydon Water, which at low tide is a vast stretch of mud with a channel marked by rows of posts and at high tide resembles a huge sea lake, past Burgh Castle, a massive ruin of the Roman Station Gariononum, a relic of the Roman occupation of Britain. The limit of navigation of the Waveney is at Geldeston Lock, a distance of 22 miles from Breydon. A dyke connects this river with Oulton Broad, which is one mile long, has an average width of half a mile,

a beautiful dyke only 1½ miles from the sea.

The Bure becomes navigable midst beautifully-wooded banks at Coltishall, 11½ miles from Norwich by rail, and five miles by water from Wroxham, "the centre of Broadland." For the first 10½ miles, until it reaches Horning Ferry Inn, the old gabled part of which dates back to the thirteenth century, its banks are bordered by thatched bungalows with well-kept lawns and flower gardens, by woods and meadows with golden buttercups and green-bordered shadowy dykes, whilst beyond to Yarmouth and the sea is mostly marsh and meadowland.

It is at Wroxham that a large number of people

Hickling Broad

and boasts the finest yacht station in East Anglia.

The river Bure and its tributaries the Thurne and the Ant are perhaps the most attractive. They have the largest number of Broads and offer the greatest scope for sailing, cruising, the naturalist, antiquarian and the fisherman. A most delightful cruise is from Potter Heigham by way of Kendal Dyke, Heigham Sound and Old Meadow Dyke to Horsey Mere. Meadow Dyke is "very lovely with a profusion of wild flowers on its banks. The channel is narrow, but the water is deep." Horsey Mere is

commence their Broadland holidays. Combined rail, motor coach and boat trips are run daily during the summer from various stations in Norfolk to Wroxham, and include a motor boat trip to Wroxham Broad, Horning and Ranworth Broad, and if time permits a visit to Ranworth Church, called the "Cathedral of the Broads," which contains beautiful carvings and probably the most ancient rood screen in the country.

Five hundred passengers from all parts of the country are dealt with at our Wroxham station every week-end during the summer months.

377